BACOPA

Literary Review 2020

Writers Alliance of Gainesville

The views expressed in this collection—whether fiction, nonfiction, poetry, or humor—are solely those of the authors and not necessarily shared by Writers Alliance of Gainesville or its members. Any aberration from editing standards or conventions are at the insistence of a work's author.

Cover Art: Oliver Keyhani
Cover/Text/Layout Design: Richard Skinner

Fonts:

Calisto MT
An old-style serif typeface designed for the Monotype Corporation foundry in 1986 by Ron Carpenter, a British typographer, Calisto MT is intended to function as a typeface for both body text and display text.

Adobe Jensen Pro
An old-style serif typeface drawn for Adobe Systems by its chief type designer Robert Slimbach, Adobe Jensen Pro's Roman styles are based on a text face cut by Nicolas Jenson in Venice around 1470; its italics are based on those created by Ludovico Vicentino degli Arrighi fifty years later.

From the Editor

Humor can provide a break or respite; it can also make difficult subjects more palatable, soften hard edges, tell a truth, release some demons, and upend expectations. Notes from The Creative Nonfiction Foundation webinar with Shannon Reed, "When Is It Okay to Laugh?"

When we decided in January to invite humor this year, we had no idea a pandemic was about to descend on us—ostensibly not at all funny, yet an opportunity to soften some very hard truths and release a variety of demons.

Our readers can look forward to "normal" humor, such as Jon Shorr's "Jesus's Bar Mitzvah Speech" and Chris Gilmore's "Mansplaining." But the demands of quarantining, and responses to daily death rate tolls, have also brought a range of humorous responses.

Stuart Stromin's "An Open Letter to the Secretary General" notes the difficulty for canines *to maintain the same enthusiasm, energy, and vigilance* given humans' recent, *more dog-like behavior*, especially their *unusual fondness for walks.*

At the other end of coronavirus humor, we have "Notes from the Editors on 'Orange is the Darkest Color'" by Cadence Mandybura, reminding us how hard it is to believe the reality of our current grim experience.

Even where there was no mention of this spring's specific difficulties, a large percent of our submissions emphasized grief, family, love of pets, and ominous foreboding. So, the accepted works this year accurately reflect what's on the minds of writers and poets everywhere.

Sarina Bosco's "An interval of time just before the onset" seems to refer to an oncoming storm, but its threatening tone (*and you wait—one, two*) implies the "storm" could take any form.

Kurt Caswell recalls *When the bomb cyclone hit west Texas, I was reading Emily Dickenson aloud to Kona, the German shepherd who shares my home.*

> To die—without the Dying
> And life—without the Life
> This is the hardest Miracle

In "Body Everywhere," Hailee Nielsen writes, *The first time I see a dead whale on the beach . . . I do not know . . . decay turns whale bodies into explosives.*

Krista, in Evan Guilford-Blake's "Dust," probes her husband's ashes with her left index finger and keeps specks of it on her finger all day. Then walking in the rain, holding her son's small hand with her right hand, *reaches out with her left and lets the water spill across it.*

Among the works that are pandemic-related, most have at least some element of optimism. David B. Maas describes, while "Getting Ready for Bed," *dismantling myself thought by thought, / until only my name remains / floating above me, trying to recall / how it knows me, this man, / this barely asleep ambassador of hope.*

From Virginia Boudreau's elegy, "Grass": *You've been gone almost eight years now . . . But still, this perfect brown bunny, on grass that's about to green, is a gift. It's a resurrection of hope in this tired world riddled with a germ that also steals breath and provides no answers.*

Facing a new normal under government-ordered quarantine, writes Virginia Watts in "The Mouth on the Mountain," *we are no longer moving on top of the earth's surfaces as we used to.* Watts recalls *traveling the Pennsylvania Turnpike in the back seat of my parents' car,* likening our current experience to being deep inside a tunnel: *Your clouds and your sky, your moon and your sun, hidden from view. Even though this is not a place you are used to, you must take this journey. There is no other way to go.*

Mary Bast

Mary Bast	Senior Editor/Creative Nonfiction
James Singer III	Associate Editor/Fiction
J.N. Fishhawk	Poetry Editor
Kaye Linden	Short-Short Editor
Stephanie Seguin	Humor Editor

Bacopa Literary Review 2020 Prizes

॰ঌ৽

FICTION
First Prize
Proxy / page 59 / James D'Angelo
Second Prize
Junk / page 10 / Siamak Vossoughi

CREATIVE NONFICTION
First Prize
Grass / page 16 / Virginia Boudreau
Second Prize
What Nightmare is This? / page 79 / Rachel Amegatcher

SHORT-SHORT
First Prize
An interval of time just before the onset / page 1 / Sarina Bosco
Second Prize
Remember the Mayflies / page 75 / Joshua Jones

POETRY
First Prize
Sacrament / page 5 / Caitlin Cacciatore
Second Prize
First Snowfall on 18th Avenue / page 23 / Patrick Cabello Hansel

HUMOR
First Prize
Jesus's Bar Mitzvah Speech / page 19 / Jon Shorr
Second Prize
Notes from the Editors on
"Orange is the Darkest Color" / page 65 / Cadence Mandybura

Contents

঵

FICTION

CREATIVE NONFICTION

SHORT-SHORT

POETRY

HUMOR

An interval of time just before the onset

Sarina Bosco

The wind, first, coming in through the open windows like a gasp. And the light on the treetops vibrant, velvet, virgin leaves unfurling to swell in the thick air.

It won't come until sleep is standing in the doorway. Draped like a woolen blanket over calves, thighs, chest, mouth, lashes drawing down against the pressure change. A rumble that stirs both fear and exhilaration. Counting *one, two;* everything damp but not yet wet. Everything on the cusp. The blades of grass turning in twilight, leaves showing their pale undersides, the wind picking up. The fine hair of the body lifting, listening.

A grumble like a father's voice far off; straining to hear it and counting *one, two.* Heavy tongue feathered against an open mouth. And just the slightest arch in the neck as though from thirst.

The trees restless, rabbits tucked away in tangles of forsythia, delicate buttercups torn in an updraft. The golden petals tumbling across lawns and warm asphalt. *One, two,* holding breath and waiting *for what?*

And then it comes so softly, at first, that it isn't even heard. Just felt as moisture rises to the surface of the skin, kin seeking kin. The sound of it in the new-minted dark a rush—each weighty patter, each—*one, two*—the light wrenching eyelids back and eardrums poised—the crack a sound of wood and water, delayed, like tragedy or purpose or fate. Everything damp *and you wait—*

one, two.

Reading Emily Dickinson to a German shepherd during the spring bomb cyclone in west Texas

Kurt Caswell

❧

In memoriam

When the bomb cyclone hit west Texas, I was reading Emily Dickinson aloud to Kona, the German shepherd who shares my house. "It will be summer—eventually," I read to her, whose ears stand so tall, and whose eyes, as she turns her head to one side to hear me, are so dark and alive and awake, even as her body is falling apart. Summer will come, but not today, not now, not yet, because this spring has been so cold, and for the past few days, wet, the coldest and wettest spring that I can remember here, and now the bomb cyclone comes running over the plain, its great winds and its great wall of dust. After two days of rain, the ground needed a few hours to dry out. That wind pushed over and pushed through for most of the day, beating out a rhythm from gust to wane until about four o'clock when the blue Texas sky—blue like Texas bluebells—went grey-dark with bomb cyclone dust, and the only thing moving on the streets were blown leaves running in packs, plastic water bottles tumbling along the curbs, and the odd plastic shopping bag, inflated and rising, rising.

Seated in front of the front window, her chin resting on the window sill, the German shepherd dog barks a howl like the wolfish German shepherd dog she is, a bark-howl song to drive off the several stray cats that range along the street and cross the street in front of her, or come up onto her front porch—the indignity of that—or pass beneath the window right under her nose. She rises so suddenly and startlingly, spinning on her old back legs that hardly work anymore, to bark and rage at the cats as the bomb cyclone gusts at sixty-eight miles per hour, snapping the branches of Siberian elm and red oak, and hurling them onto the street, bending to breaking a few power poles, lifting the trailer of a semi northbound for Amarillo and twisting it like a pig's tail, and so "swept the World away—".

She's a good dog, and an old dog now—her black face gone all grey-dark—but when faced with cats, she's a pup all over again.

Poor Kona. What happens to a German shepherd and her hips and back legs: the strength that once propelled her on a coyote-run across the mesquite-covered Llano Estacado has drained away, and she can hardly rise from her own bed now, the rear left leg—weaker than the right—and the left foot caught beneath the right foot, and twisted a little on her leg, so that stepping on her own foot she knocks herself down while trying to get up. And getting up, she totters, sways, hesitates, then gets her steady-on only to flop down somewhere else on the slick hardwood floor that makes rising even more a thing she can hardly do. When we make one of our several daily walks together—short, brief, a cruise around the block—she doesn't really want to walk anymore, but she does want to sniff, and then in her beauty she is sniffing, catching a scent plume on the air, nosing out the measure of the ground, her world, but her legs don't want to hold her long so not so far from the house at all she lies down on a neighbor's tidy grass. "To die—takes just a little while," I read in Dickinson, but not to be morose, as thrust into this world as she is—Dickinson and the German shepherd dog—she happily appears in it, and as she is in it, she's in it to ride it out as well as the body will ride it: "I am alive—I guess— . . . How good—to be alive!"

So despite the bomb cyclone—"The Happy Winds—" and the cold of these past days, it is spring in west Texas and in spring time, the cardinal arrives again at my bird bath, the shallow stone depression I clean and fill. Two cardinals come, a mated pair, arriving so suddenly and gaudily as if from a nowhere place to grace a limb in the red oak just leafing out and the crepe myrtle and on the fence-top to sing a red-flashed morning song to melt the heart at the ear's expense.

Oh Kona-dog, sweet, watching the birds at play in the branches, musing about your younger days, read Dickinson—this—aloud:

> God gave a loaf to every bird—
> But just a crumb—to me—

I will miss her, when she is gone, and even as she is not gone, I miss her. I wonder. I worry. I think on her leaving me, or me not leaving with her as she leaves, and wondering how may I avoid it? There is no avoiding it, no chance to live forever—her or me—so how to live without the dying and the undying hurt that comes in losing what we love best? I read in Dickinson:

> To die—without the Dying
> And live—without the Life
> This is the hardest Miracle

But there is no way, no path, no magic that will perform this hardest miracle, except in accepting another kind of loss:

> Me from myself—to banish—
> Had I Art—
>
> . . .
> How this be
> Except by Abdication—
> Me—of Me?

No, not that, sweet Kona-dog. Not to banish or abdicate the self—by Art or any other otherwise—because the darkest secret is that Art but affirms loss—this only, is—that we awaken loss in our Art to know we live. Instead of abdication, I must walk this road with you, you with me: in spring, I read Emily Dickinson to a German shepherd as the bomb cyclone rages. I read it aloud, loud—as the great winds carry the grey dust from the dry ground up into that Texas blue sky—still blue above the grey—then down, down in fine raiment to fall and pepper every little thing—Kona-dog and me—where our feeble legs carry us along, in our meekness, our temporary forms—for now—to roam, to explore, to wander together our way to the end, me—of her, her—of me.

Sacrament

Caitlin Cacciatore

For M.G.

The work of mourning is never done.
There is no timetable to clock out,
No neat and tidy shifts after which
I can return to a place of safety and rest;
No foreman watches me, and since you asked,
No funeral was held.
We have long since done away
With wearing black in times like these.
My toils mean so little;
Everyone, now, writes a eulogy here,
A dirge there—the world is laid to rest in a shroud;
A fog of uncertainty lingers long into the twilight hours.
I suppose I should say, "It's no trouble at all,"
Or even, "It's a labor of love," but I don't want to lie
In an elegy. This task is Promethean;
It binds me, and I, like Atlas,
Must hold the weight of the disappearing world
On shoulders too narrow for such a task;
You would think the load grows lighter,
But you'd be wrong—
All those souls; all that sorrow,
It weighs too heavily upon us all.
I wish I could have taken a warship
And set you out to sea at its prow,
Your pyre so bright for one shining moment
That someone, somewhere
Might mistake it for a star.

The Movieteller

Yongsoo Park

The first movie my parents took my brother and me to see in America was *Conan the Barbarian,* which starred Arnold Schwarzenegger as a slave-turned-warrior. My parents, who hadn't ever been to the movies in America either and didn't know what an R-rating meant, chose that movie because the poster hanging outside the theater made it look like an adventure cartoon for children.

I'm not sure when it dawned on them that the movie wasn't what they'd signed us up for. But when slave girls appeared in the nude, and then Conan started having sex with a witch who turned into a streaming fireball that darted back-and-forth across the screen, I knew that this movie was very special and infinitely better than all the movies I'd seen back in South Korea.

There, my father had regularly taken me to our run-down neighborhood theater, and I'd seen more sappy Korean melodramas and martial arts movies from Hong Kong, all standard late-1970s fare, than any little kid anywhere ought to have seen. But kung fu movies were harmless fun even with their stylized violence, and thanks to strict government censorship, Korean melodramas were always very tame. Most were about penniless orphans who were eventually reunited with a rich distant relative. Suffice to say, nothing I'd seen in Korea had prepared me for the wonders of *Conan the Barbarian.*

After the movie finally ended, my parents got up from their seats, and we all filed out of the theater in silence. They never spoke to us about the experience afterwards, and my brother and I didn't ask any questions. In hindsight, I can fully understand my parents' decision not to have a heart-to-heart with us about what we'd just seen. They were very modest people who'd come of age during the Korean War and had soaked up the mores of a very socially conservative society. So it was only natural that they carried on as if nothing unusual had just occurred and hoped that my brother and I would somehow forget everything we'd seen. This was, of course, something we couldn't do. The movies, especially rated-R ones, called to me, and I had to get my fix.

So I turned to Willie, the boy king of our street. Two years older than me and already an old-hand at navigating life, he had personally given me a master class on every curse word there was in English and even some in Espanol when I'd first moved to the block. I knew that he regularly snuck into rated-R movies, and I begged him to take me with him. At first, he refused because he insisted I looked too little and would only be a hindrance to him. But then, after I shot up a few inches and put on some weight over the summer, he finally gave in.

So on a cool Saturday just a few weeks after the start of fifth grade, I went with him and two other older boys from our block to the Jackson, our go-to theater, with three dollars in my pocket--two for admission to the matinee and another dollar to buy chips and candy to smuggle inside.

Willie's method for getting past the theater's defenses was simple. He just went up to random grown-ups waiting in line outside the theater and asked them to take us in with them. A lot of people gave us funny looks and said no. But after five no's, the sixth person he asked just chuckled and said, "Sure, kid. Why not?"

And just like that we had our new guardian buy our tickets for us and walked right in as if we were one big happy blended family. And just like that, a world of forbidden pleasures was opened to me.

I graduated from Willie's program and regularly went to the movies on my own. And the wholesome programming I'd received in South Korea was quickly replaced by a different kind of programming from cinematic gems such as *Zapped*, *Private School*, *Joysticks*, *My Tutor*, and *Losin' It,* all teenage sexploitation movies calculated to appeal to prurient young men.

By the sixth grade, my movie-going experience was catapulted to a whole new level when Oscar, an older boy from my block, became the usher at the Jackson. Thanks to this inside connection, I no longer had to even scrounge about for a genial adult to get me into the theater. All I needed was two bucks for the ticket, and Oscar, the gatekeeper, let me in to whatever movie I wanted to see.

Having ready-access to rated-R movies won me a lot of cachet from my peers, who were at that age when hormones were doing crazy things to our bodies and minds. At school, while girls in my class surreptitiously passed around dog-eared copies of Judy Blume's *Forever* to share knowledge about budding sexuality, the boys in my class came to me, the self-educated authority on such matters from having diligently studied the canon of early 1980s American teenage sex comedies which were at their peak.

Boys huddled around me at recess as I held court and re-told the stories of the latest movies to hit the screens. In these schoolyard movie rebroad-casts, I honed my craft. I learned to trim, embellish, and to hurry to the meat of the story. I utilized parallel cutting, flashbacks, and flash forwards. I adjusted the pace of my storytelling to fit the action, sometimes lavishing ten minutes on key scenes that took a mere thirty seconds in the movie. And as I gained more confidence in my storytelling, I took liberties and took the story to places that veered from the original to better meet the particular tastes of my audience. Such improvisation was, in fact, my first stab at creating my own stories.

My reign as the unofficial raconteur of rated-R movies lasted just about a year. By the following September when I started junior high school, many kids had gotten cable TV and VCRs, which both opened up a slew of programming that had previously been available only at the movies. My services as a movieteller to a prurient prepubescent set were no longer needed. So like artisan weavers and scribes from earlier eras, I, too, was made obsolete by technology, at the ripe age of twelve.

But it was a good run while it lasted. Sneaking into rated-R movies was something that went against everything that I'd been taught as a boy in South Korea. It was categorically unwholesome, borderline delinquent, and definitely not something any model child would have done. But doing so at that particular point in the analog era was a defining experience for me, and it came at a time in my life when I needed something to help me fit in and find validation. And it did those things and more. It drove me to be a storyteller of my own and helped shape the proud odd grown-up that I eventually became.

The Episcopalian Church car park

Stephanie Powell

Mustafa sells kebabs from a truck in the Episcopalian Church car park. On hot days he cannot tell the difference between the fryer and his flesh. Sweat travels from the creases of his elbows to his palms. Souped-up Commodores and Fiestas roll in and out of the KFC drive-through across the road. The snarl of high-powered engines and smell of fried chicken penetrate four lanes of traffic between them. Mustafa waits. He prepares slices of tomato and onion. He keeps an eye on the oil boiling deep in its vat. He tends to the meat, rotating on a metal skewer, like a newborn. Religiously checking its temperature and pampering its smooth, moist skin. At midday his regulars appear for lunch. Sunburned tradies who are building units on freshly bulldozed lots. Modern, cubic homes for up-and-coming middle class families. A full shawarma with extra chilli. The pharmacist from the chemist comes on days he doesn't bring a packed lunch. A lamb donner wrap and a can of fanta. Later, older boyfriends with hatchbacks bring their high school girlfriends for half-chips, before retiring to empty houses for a few secretive hours. Mustafa shuffles up and down the small gangway, between counter and fryer. The till rings on and off, vehicles speed towards the entrance of the highway. When the sun sets, the giant cross behind the truck lights up. A beacon calling to the hungry and devout. Mustafa works into the night, until the lights on the strip start to disappear.

FICTION SECOND PRIZE
Junk
Siamak Vossoughi

About once a week we'd get a call from somebody asking us to haul their junk, and they'd call their junk what anybody with the sense God gave them would call it, which was *junk*. So I was entirely unprepared when I got a call for some hauling out in Duven and the guy said he had a truckload of stuff but he didn't want to call it junk.

"It's my parents' stuff," he said. "I don't want it, but it's not junk. They both died."

"Okay. You want us to haul it away?"

"Yes. But it's not junk."

"All right. It's not junk. But you do want it hauled away?"

"Yes."

I made a plan to go out there Wednesday and I told Louis about it. He looked up from his phone. He put his phone away in his pocket.

"He said that?" he said.

"Yes."

"Tell me everything he said."

"I just told you."

"Tell it slowly."

I told him again slowly.

"He's right. It's not junk," Louis said.

"What is it then?"

"He said his parents both died, didn't he?"

"That doesn't mean it's not junk."

"You don't understand. You haven't lost a mother or father."

"Neither have you. I saw them at Christmas."

"But I think about it a lot. Anyway, he's right. It's not junk." He looked me up and down. "We shouldn't wear our T-shirts when we go out there."

"What the hell is wrong with our T-shirts?"

"It says Tree Service and Hauling Junk."

"Because that's what we do."

"We can go without them for one day."

"I designed the shirts."

"It's a good design. But if it's not junk, we shouldn't wear them."

"I'm going to go load the truck," I said.

I went out back and loaded the truck for the afternoon. We had a tree job over on Greenwood. I thought about all the time I spent designing the shirts. I hadn't half-assed it. It was a good shirt and I liked putting it on in the morning.

I went back inside.

"What are you going to do about the truck?"

"What about it?"

"It says We Haul Junk on the side. Because, as I mentioned, that's what we do."

Louis had a look of panic. We went outside to look at the truck.

"I painted that on," I said.

"I know."

"We can't not bring the truck."

"I know."

Louis stared at the side of the truck.

"He said his mother and father *both* died?"

"Yes."

"And the stuff is their stuff?"

"Yes."

He looked through the stack of wood and cardboard back there and pulled out a piece of cardboard.

"You still have the paint?"

"Yes. In the shed."

He went to the shed and got the paint and a brush. He set it on the back of the truck and began painting the cardboard. He kept coming around to the side of the truck and looking at the sign to make it match. When he finished, he showed me. He placed it over the word *junk*.

"We Haul Stuff?" I said.

"Yes. Just for Wednesday. And we'll have this around in case anybody else doesn't want to call their stuff junk."

I didn't like it. I didn't care so much about the shirts, but I didn't like the idea of changing around the whole idea of what we did. You were supposed to pick something and stay with it. I didn't like the idea of changing things around every time somebody didn't like a word.

"You know," I said, "every piece of junk we've hauled was probably once owned by somebody who died."

Louis thought it over. "We've hauled a lot of old junk."

"So does that mean it wasn't junk? You look at it like that and *nothing* is junk. Even if it's obviously a piece of junk."

"Maybe nothing *is* junk," Louis said.

"Jesus," I said. "Maybe we should change our T-shirts then. Maybe they should say Tree Service And Hauling Junk That Is Only Junk If Everybody Is Alive And Kicking."

I went in and got my hat and we drove over to Greenwood. We didn't say much in the truck.

"Not everything was once by owned by somebody who died," Louis said.

"What?"

"Not everything was owned by somebody who died. New stuff isn't like that."

"New stuff isn't junk. That's the whole point of it being new."

When we got there, I went up in the tree. Even if a tree isn't too high off the ground, it's a good place to sit and think. I was trying to figure out what bothered me about the whole thing, and it felt like when I have a fight with Maggie over some little thing, and then it felt like what bothered me was that he was right. And that bothered me even more.

"Nobody's going to do this for us, you know," I called from the tree.

Louis was cleaning up the shoots.

"What?"

"Nobody's going to do this for us when our parents go."

"We can do our own hauling."

"Not that. I mean nobody who's a *stranger* is going to worry about how we feel. They're going to say, okay, sorry about your parents, but here's our job, this is what we do. These are the words we use for our job and we can't change the words when somebody dies because a lot of people have died and we can't change the words every time that happens because we'd be changing the words all the time. That's what they're going to say. I just want you to know. I just want you to be ready for when you're on the other side of it."

"We're the strangers?" Louis said.

"Of course we're the strangers. Do you know anyone in Duven?"

"It doesn't feel like we're strangers."

"Well, we are." I cut through a thick shoot. I cut it thinking that if it hit Louis on the head, I wouldn't be too upset.

Just then I remembered about our receipts. On the receipts we gave it said Tree Service and Hauling Junk too. No sir, I thought. I'm not going to say a word. One little word like that on one little piece of paper? It was no way to live. I tried to think about all the times we'd hauled junk away from a house where somebody had just died. Who were we? We were just the junk haulers. We didn't know them. Jesus Christ. I almost wanted *Louis* to remember about the receipts so I could holler at him about it. I couldn't bring it up *and* holler at him about it.

No sir, I thought. I've got to draw a line somewhere.

I worked on the shoots high up that were hardest to reach.

I kept thinking about it all the time up in the tree and I wondered if there was a way I could've told Louis about the job when the guy had first called without mentioning that he didn't want us to call his parents' stuff junk. Who expects a guy to run with it like that?

I was still thinking about it that night in bed, until Maggie asked me what was wrong and I said it was nothing. But I was still thinking about it the next day when we were working some trees up the road, and I kept seeing the word 'junk' on the receipt and thinking about the guy tomorrow seeing it, and thinking about his mother and father, who I didn't know from a can of paint.

It wouldn't take much to change it. It was a hell of a lot easier than hanging the piece of cardboard over the side of the truck. But that wasn't the point. The point was that if you kept getting smaller and smaller down to the tiniest details like that, when would you ever stop? A man went to somebody's house where people had died and said, Sorry to hear about your parents, and loaded the junk and hauled it away. That's it and that's all.

When I got in Wednesday morning, Louis had already rigged the word Stuff over where it said Junk. He did a pretty good job of it, I have to admit. He didn't say anything as we drove over there and I wondered if he *had* remembered and was waiting to see if I would say something. That wasn't like him, but then again I hadn't seen him do everything he could to not mention junk like this either.

"Goddammit," I said finally. "You win. We have to change the receipts."

"What?"

"The receipts say junk on them. If you're going to give him a receipt, you might as well cross out the word junk and write something else there too," I said. "Jesus Christ."

He looked like he might cry. "Thanks, Mike," he said.

"What are you thanking me for? *Your* parents are fine. Your father is as grouchy as ever and your mother is the only one who can stomach him."

"I know," he said. "But I think about their death a lot."

When we got to the guy's house, Louis fixed the receipt to it didn't say junk on it. That was the final piece. I got out and took in the morning air. No junk anywhere in sight. No junk anywhere for miles.

We went to work.

Getting Ready for Bed

David B. Maas

I unlace my left shoe
and kick off worries about humanity's doom.
Then the right shoe lands
and I start to forget any math problems
that might have recently come up.
My belt slides onto the floor, while I
lose sight of cracks in the walls
of the elementary school downtown.
I wonder how my neighbors
are paying their hospital bills
after their insurance dropped them.
As my pants fall
I no longer recollect their faces
or which of them is unemployed.
I shed my shirt, slip into bed
wearing T-shirt, boxers, socks
which I might peel away and throw on top of
questions about doing the laundry,
scrubbing the bathroom, paying the rent,
leaving out water for the cat
(who obsesses over impossible objects
but manages to sleep anytime).
I might keep my socks on after all,
not care whether I left food in the sink.
I disremember turning off lights or the oven
or locking the front door.
The darkness grows bright,
dismantling myself, thought by thought,
until only my name remains
floating above me, trying to recall
how it knows me, this man,
this barely asleep ambassador of hope.

Grass

Virginia Boudreau

His chocolate coat, his long ears, his sweet silhouette are all anticipation hovering on a bed of Easter grass. His basket is this clearing in the glow of earliest morning . . . and it's all in my front yard. I marvel at the serendipity of seeing a bunny over by the stone wall, this day of all days. It's a treat, particularly at a time when the Covid-19 virus holds the world captive, and nothing seems certain anymore.

I stand on the lawn, not quite green. It's mostly a spread of dull sienna grass, littered with twigs and pine needles, worn thin in places and stitched with smatterings of sheep sorrel and hawkweed. The rabbit sits still as can be but for his twitchy ears, shell pink and gleaming, translucent in the wan light. They are impossibly delicate and fill me with wonder. He pauses for one perfect moment before startling into the tangle of juniper edging the driveway.

I study the cushion of celadon moss on the bank. The rock border at the top is starting to crumble; only a web of honeysuckle vines holds it together. Soon, it will be bathed in a heaven of gold and plum petals, but not yet. There are a few pools of limp and wrinkled leaves, hinting at the foxgloves that will spike to sway under the June sun.

We lie in the field out on the bluff, arms pillowing our heads as we follow the parade of cumulous mounds in the sky. They look as plush and inviting as the feather tick we used to bounce on. "Remember jumping on that old mattress 'til your mom would holler up the stairs?" We giggle, recalling the goose down that drifted like dandelion fluff through the dusty attic with the window high up in the eaves.

The beauty around us is so intense it seems frivolous and the smell in the air could make you dizzy if you let it. The lushness of early summer conjures a heady mix of wild berries and roses and leaf shadow. Lupine spritz a haze of lavender and puffballs release delicate filaments to ride random breezes. We delight in watching them hover and sail, predicting how far they'll fly. "You can make wishes on those you know?" Your voice is quiet.

I laugh but don't say I wish on everything going these days. I try hard not to hear the sound of your breathing; it makes me think of you, stretching and grabbing for air like apple pickers teetering to reach the ripest fruit on the highest branches. How many times have I held the sweetness of a small perfect world in my hands and taken it for granted?

As the rabbit fades into the thicket, I picture us sprawled in the long grass. Daisies were everywhere, mingling like leggy girls in fluttering white skirts, dancing like there was no tomorrow. We wove chains for our hair, plucked petals for hours, saying "He loves me, he loves me not . . ." and we wouldn't stop until we ended up with the answer we wanted.

You've been gone almost eight years now, and I never did get my wish. But still, this perfect brown bunny, on grass that's about to green, is a gift. It's a resurrection of hope in this tired world riddled with a germ that also steals breath and provides no answers. I like to think he's a symbol for all we cannot see but trust in, anyway.

For now, it's enough to know that new shoots will again push at ceilings of mussed soil to blink tenderly in renewed light. And, blossoms readying to veil gnarled limbs will later burst into the fullness of their bounty, as they always have. I need to think that's what happened for you; and that this small, soft creature is letting us know, by his presence this day, that it will be the same for us when our own time comes.

Buriers

Rachel Poteet

When all but John had gone from You,
Mary, Mary, other names I can't recall
The ninth hour; no time for embalming,
For eye-stones, soft damp cloths, stitching, funeral makeup
Whether you pressed against the phalanx
Carrying Him first to a mass grave
Or whether you caught in your arms the falling cross—
Once my mother buried a chick she caught falling from a branch—
Levered the nails from his feet
Salvaging where they had torn that temple down
Did you send John, white-faced, to make excuses to a centurion who could
only nod and mumble prayer in an unfamiliar tongue?
Once I buried a ring on a mountaintop and cried tears in unfamiliar
shapes—
Did John, silent, take in his arms the dull-eyed God?
Light from empty-bellied hours
Could Mary tear her eyes from Your feet?
Calloused, road-rough, pierced
Legs wet with blood and shit, did she know
She would come back to You, greatest
Of all Magi bearing gifts, arms laid with spices
When they laid You, blood-bloated,
On the cloth in the garden—
My friend buried her child under a butterfly bush—
How many layers of cloth did it take?
How many did You have, God-abandoned God,
Buried Son, buried by women,
Rolling their sleeves up to carry You beneath an arch of stone?
A stranger buried her son's ashes, my love's ashes, under a stone bridge—
Day-blind, they carried You,
Stinking and glorious, my God, my God, buried Your corpse
Like a mustard seed
In the grave.

Jesus's Bar Mitzvah Speech

Jon Shorr

[recently translated from a parchment titled *The Chronicle of Eliphaz*, found sealed in an earthenware vessel in a cave above the Sea of Galilee]

[1] And it came to pass that the people entered the temple, many of them late, and waited through much standing and sitting and standing and sitting until finally the scrolls had been carried among the people and read. And Jesus stood before the people and spoke unto them, saying:

[2] "When I was little, me and my mom and [air quotes] "dad" lived in Egypt for a while before we moved back here to Nazareth. And it was no walk in the park, apparently, more like a walk in the Negev. Then after we got there, the people were nice enough, but I was always afraid of something terrible happening: frogs falling out of the sky or some mongo hail storm or a really gross case of zits or scabies or something. But my mom used to tell me to try not to get worried. And my dad would tell me to try not to turn on to problems that upset me, that everything would be all right.

[3] "So guess what: In today's Torah portion, Pharaoh refuses to let the Israelites leave Egypt, even after the first seven plagues. Is that a coincidence or what! You can only imagine my surprise a couple years ago when Rabbi Jechonias told me my Torah portion was about the plagues! Maybe I'd just heard it in shul when I was a baby, or maybe it's some kind of ancestral memory. Whatever it was, it begat me to really buckle down and study it."

[4] And the people in the temple listened to Jesus, except for Mrs. Silverblatt who was upset with her son for wearing non-matching sandals, and Jesus spoketh thus.

[5] "There'd be these plagues, and Pharaoh's all omigod boils, make 'em go away, and Moses goes, "No problem, just let my people go," and Pharaoh's like, "Sure, just make it stop," so God stops the plague, and then Pharaoh's just like, "I don't remember saying you could go!" and then it was just back to building pyramids again."

[6] And the multitudes nodded their heads, some in affirmation, some in an attempt to stay awake. And Jesus spoketh thus.

[7] "I can really relate to this parsha because sometimes my mom and my [air quotes] "dad" want me to do stuff, and I'm like, so if I do this stuff, will you let me go over Jude's house and play, and they say ok, so I do it, but then they're like "it's getting dark," or I didn't do my homework, or we have to get ready for Shabbos or something, and I'm like, but you said, and then the next time I want to do something, Dad'll say sure, soon as you sharpen the saws or level these table legs or something."

[8] And all the while his mother vacillated between pride and wishing for an out of body experience, Jesus spoketh thus.

[9] "In my Maftir was the line *Veyad'u Mitsrayim ki-ani Adonay bintoti et-yadi al-Mitsrayim vehotseti et-beney-Yisra'el mitocham.* 'When I display My power and bring the Israelites out from among them, Egypt will know that I am God.' When I first read it, I was thinking Moses said it, and I'm like who's he think he is, calling himself God, but then I remembered my [air quotes] "dad" when we were getting ready to come back to Nazareth, and He said something that this reminded me of, but I can't remember it exactly, but then I realized it was actually God talking, and I thought, well, yeah, easy for you to say, but based on Pharaoh bailing even after all those plagues, don't count on it."

[10] And some of the people understood, and others understood not the saying that he spake unto them. And others asked of him from where his wisdom cometh. And he answereth and saith unto them thus:

[11] "I'd like to thank Cantor Melchior for helping me learn to chant my Torah portion. We worked for three years; it seemed like thirty. There were days when I was really inspired and others when I was just sad and tired, but he stuck with me, and I only hope I've met if not exceeded his expectations.

[12] "I'd like to thank Dr. Balthazar and the Brotherhood for the Kiddush cup and prayerbook. And not to seem ungrateful, but even though I'm a *man* now, I really don't like the taste of wine and I don't think the congregation should be y'know pushing kids to drink, I guess I only want to say that If there's a way, take this cup away from me, well, maybe not the actual cup, but if you could wash it out really well, so when I'm drinking goat milk or something, it won't taste like poison.

[13] "I'd like to thank Mrs. Caspar and the Sisterhood for the congregational luncheon after services today. And it's not just bread alone; there'll be egg salad, too. I hope you'll remember me when you eat and drink. In another 20 years or so, when I'm older and really a [air quotes] "man," I hope you'll let me repay the honor by coming to my house for dinner.

[14] "I'd like to thank Judas's dad for driving the guys over in his chariot. Andy, Pete, Jimmy, Bart, Phil, Matt, Jude, thanks for putting up with my whining about mid-week Hebrew school.

[15]"Most of all, I'd like to thank my parents: Mom, [air quotes] "Dad," you're the greatest; I couldn't have made it to this day without you.

[16] "And finally, Grandpa Jake, I'll write you my first thank you note with the fountain reed you gave me."

[17]And the multitudes dispersed, some to the Ahazariah and Peninah Plotnik multipurpose room for luncheon and others to the Nazareth Tech-Mt. Tabor game.

Body Everywhere

Hailee Nielsen

The first time I see a dead whale on the beach, I am ten years old and still breathing through California lungs. Imagine it as a church, body as temples torn from bodies of water. Ghosts wide enough to step into. I follow Turner toward it as the three of us (whale, girl, dog) catch in the wind and shift. I do not know at the time that decay turns whale bodies into explosives. Barnacles or mold. I wonder as vomit asks to etch patterns on the back of my teeth. After his inspection, Turner lifts his leg on the baleen bristles. We walk up the shore to the road to the house, where I force syllables through picket fence slats shaped like "it's okay, I'm not hungry, Mom will be back soon." Where I fall asleep and imagine ripples of breath across whale rib cages. The next day, the dark shape collapses in on itself, all gravity and tattered skin draped over bone. The blubber hangs in the pines for weeks.

First Snowfall on 18th Avenue

Patrick Cabello Hansel

The last leaves of the Norway maple
refused to turn this fall, refused to fall
down. Now their green fingers welcome
the first flakes as fur. The ground begins,
like a dog, to sniff out this new arrival
it vaguely remembers: is it friend or
foe, rival or possible mate. Like
other years, other snows, the grass
remembers that it knows how to surrender.

The pile of leaves that Talia has not
yet bagged begin to cotton up, and
across the street, the toddler's broken
trike sports crooked white wings.
Evening slides into night, and the solar
lawn lights begin to flicker under
their silken veils. We sit with our tea,
on the porch. As the hours pass,
quiet settles over the city like a
calming womb: to drive, to shout,
to summon sirens or a gunshot
would be blasphemy. The divine
has come to breathe us down,
attended by angels who sing without
opening their mouths. This snow
will need to be manhandled tomorrow:
the car unstuck, the walks made
passable. But as we linger, and though
we shiver, the white, starlit dust of our
beginning and of our end eases us up
and towards bed. Sleep is snow's

sacred balm to the wide world.
Kiss upon kiss will fall upon us
throughout the long hours.
Let us breathe.

For Our Youth

Krystal Song

2018 January 12. Nakamura Himari trudged through the snow, grocery bags in one hand, cane in the other. She planned to make tonjiru soup and tofu tonight, enough for two. One serving for tonight, one serving for tomorrow's breakfast. After breakfast, there would be more decisions to be made. She would spend an hour at the Taka Market ten kilometers away, thinking through all the possible meals she could make. In five days, on Sunday, her neighbor Akari would come visit, and Himari would prepare a feast.

The streets were empty before her, the snow unmarred like a baby's skin. Kondo's population size was miniscule even for Aomori Prefecture—a mere 1,783 permanent residents. Occasionally, the town received lost tourists who strayed too far south from Mount Osore. On those rare occasions Himari was proud to show them the tiny origami museum in downtown Kondo, which housed the world's smallest paper cranes in history, folded by a young lady named Yui. Yui was still in her early thirties, but altogether spoke too loudly and dressed too scantily, especially in the freezing winter temperatures, though Himari's son had always contested she was really too old-fashioned. Perhaps Himari was old-fashioned. At seventy-one, there really wasn't any other fashion to be had.

She dusted the snow off her boots before stepping inside, changing into her house slippers. There was no mail waiting for her from the postman, no letter from her son or even the local grocery chain. Her son Sora was too busy to visit, call, or write. He had tried to get her a cellular phone years ago, but she'd protested then that she was too old to waste such money on, and couldn't he better spend the funds on his four-year-old daughter, who would soon need to attend private school? Himari's granddaughter would receive the education she had failed to provide for her son, who grew up in rural Kondo and never even heard of the *Center Shiken* exams until he entered middle school. By then it was too late, and so he did not graduate from university until he was in his late thirties, working several jobs to offset his American student tuition. Himari was proud of him, but she also never wished this for him. Who would manage Nakamura's Convenience, not to mention the vegetable garden on their three-acre property? What good was a living son who was little more than a memory, one that rippled and wavered whenever touched, like a still body of water?

He had promised her: After I graduate, I will come home and care for you. I will continue Father's legacy and run Nakamura's Convenience. I will return to Kondo and support the town, which is my home, forever.

Her son always had a way with words. An empty way with words, which served him in advertising, if not in familial relations.

Graduation day came, and a visit home did not come. Instead, a new girlfriend entered the picture, a sweet Japanese American girl named Aoi with eyes like crescent moons and wispy bangs like the fringe of an *ori* weaving. Himari pored over the photos sent in the mail, mounting them in frames in the living room.

Nakamura's Convenience can wait, she wrote. I will manage on my own until you return.

Then the wedding happened. Aoi wanted a beach ceremony, Sora wrote on a postcard, after the fact. Hawaii was beautiful in winter and very warm. We missed you. We will come visit soon.

Soon was a subjective word and Himari's interpretation of it changed daily. She developed the nervous habit of looking out the kitchen window whenever the northbound train blared its horn, the train that crossed over from Tokyo. Few passengers ever got off, and those that lingered on the platform hardly ever bore a passing resemblance to her son. When they did, she retreated to her bedroom, the only windowless room in the house, her heart pounding, her hands quivering, trying not to wait and listen for that telltale crunch of snow, footsteps on the walkway, a knock at the door.

The doorway remained empty.

She received a letter in the mail weeks later. Work had picked up in the spring. Sora was now at an advertising firm in Baltimore, a few miles from his alma mater. Money's tight, he wrote. But I'm saving up. As soon as I pass this round of layoffs, I'll make the trip overseas. I can bring Aoi. She's dying to meet you.

Himari was in her sixties now and Nakamura's Convenience wasn't what it once was. The shelves were only ever partially stocked, and layers of dust had begun accumulating on the counters. The locals never complained about the slow service, but the occasional visitor balked at the wait times and expired products. One afternoon that summer, a customer asked for a different ramen flavor. It wasn't on the shelf, but Himari knew there might be a few extras in the back. She asked him to wait just one minute as she looked through storage. When she returned, she didn't know how much time had passed. The light was setting, the customer gone, the door ajar, and Himari stood there, alone, holding the package of ramen with both hands, breathing in the faint scent of dust and mold, which she could hardly smell anymore.

Several years later the town mayor paid a visit to Nakamura's Convenience, asking Himari to kindly retire. He proposed a transfer—the town council could oversee the store and hire a manager in her place. Neighbor Megumi is only in his fifties, the mayor explained. He's better equipped to run Nakamura's Convenience. Perhaps we'll call it Kondo's Convenience, eh? Has a nicer ring to it. More punchy.

Himari nodded but could not bring herself to speak.

We want you to rest and care for your health, the mayor said. Where is your son? Didn't you say he was coming home soon? Tickets from America are truly pricey these days. Over 100,000 yen!

By this time, Sora had been gone for over sixteen years. When Himari tried to conjure his face in her memory, all she could recall were the photos sent in the mail, and the occasional Facebook posts her neighbor Akari showed her when she visited. Her son wore expensive western clothing now, his hair cut and styled like a soldier's. His complexion was paler and his cheekbones gaunter. He looked nothing like his mother or father. He looked nothing like Kondo at all.

Her letter was brief, to the point. Nakamura's Convenience, which had been her husband's crowning achievement, was leaving the family. Sora wrote back three months later. His apologies were equally brief, leaving way for a footnote at the end regarding a new granddaughter. Her sorrows slid away immediately, like the brief, flinching pain of a stubbed toe. She sent him some of her welfare money, in congratulations. He sent it back immediately, along with more.

I hear your son's doing quite well these days, Yui exclaimed, upon seeing Himari at the origami museum. Yui was now married but still dressed like a little girl. Sora had always had a soft spot for her.

He's well, Himari replied, thank you.

His business is just booming, Yui continued. Those startups are all the rage these days. Maybe even Soft Bank will invest. They just have billions and billions.

The banks Himari had visited in her youth all bore hard exteriors, steel and glass, but for her son she imagined a bank made of cotton pillows, fluffy and soft as a baby's cheek. She hoped this soft bank would invest in her son's life; she felt he needed more comfort and relaxation these days.

She stopped asking Sora to visit in her letters. She looked forward only to neighbor Akari's weekly visits, always on Sunday. Akari would bring gossip from the next town over; she would look up Sora on her Facebook account; she would show her the photos on her mobile device. How beautiful your grandchildren are! How lucky you are, Himari, to have such a big family.

Only, the ghosts were plentiful too, and they were pressing in.

At night the temperatures would drop below freezing and Himari would shiver violently on the tatami mats, her blankets rough and threadbare. She would stare up at the wooden rafters and wonder about her husband, where he was in the night sky, but more often about Sora, and where he was on the dark earth. She imagined his wife, his two daughters, his pet kitten. She wondered if his kids knew her name, if he mentioned Kondo at all, or if he merely hoped to wipe off his humbler origins like dead leaves pruned at the end of winter.

As a little boy, Sora's greatest skill was cleaning. He loved Ito's Speedy Detergent, with its artificial lemon scent—there was no smell he loved more. He would spray the windows down from top to bottom, then wipe down the glass with his reedy arms raised high, swinging back and forth like the windshield wipers of a car. She always stocked Ito's even after he left, though she never met anyone who liked the sugary lemon as he did. When she thought of that scent now, she thought of him, and she thought of his talent in wiping away what once was.

Nearly twenty-one years after her son left Kondo, on 2018 January 12, Himari went to bed around her usual time of 8:45 pm. Sometime between midnight and one in the morning, she heard a sound outside—a baby's cry, or a ghost's wail. She thought perhaps it was her son who had come after all, a moment of remembrance, a final filial act. She rushed to the door but forgot the logs of firewood Akari had stacked by the entrance. Her foot caught against the wood, and she fell forward, her chin striking the kami-dana shrine by the entrance. The door swung open, always unlocked, because Himari had never believed in unwanted visitors. Flurries of snow drifted in through the open doorway. Her brain slowed, numbed by the piercing cold. She thought of her idiot son, who was never coming after all, and of all his broken promises and empty words. She thought of the child she had raised, and mourned his loss, because the son she knew was dead after all.

* * *

NAKAMURA HIMARI, 71, WAS FOUND DECEASED IN HER ANCESTRAL HOME ON 2018 JANUARY 13, BY HER NEIGHBOR WATANABE AKARI. CAUSE OF DEATH: HYPOTHERMIA.

Nakamura Sora folds the newspaper article back into its labeled envelope, then clips it to the front of his open notebook. He stares at his clumsy handwriting, his last words marred by smudged ink. *"She thought of the child she had raised . . . "*

The truth is, he doesn't know if his mother died at midnight or one in the morning. He doesn't know if she died in the night at all. He doesn't know her final thoughts or if she even thought at all. What on earth compelled her to move blindly through the dark, without a candle or even a flashlight, to open the door at such an hour? Did she hear a stranger's cry for help? Was it a bad dream? What made her open that door? And why the fuck didn't she wait for him to help her?

Because he was never coming.

Sora closes his eyes, resisting the urge to tear his third draft into tiny paper shreds, the fates of draft one and two. He reads it once more:

"Nakamura Himari trudged through the snow, grocery bags in one hand, cane in the other. She planned to make ~~tonjiru soup and tofu tonight~~, enough for two. One serving for tonight, one serving for tomorrow's breakfast."

But his mother preferred corn potage soup, didn't she? Corn potage and leeks.

"Nakamura Himari trudged through the snow, grocery bags in one hand, cane in the other. She planned to make corn potage and leeks tonight, enough for two."

Sora books a flight for the funeral. He pays for every expense, from the kaimyo name to the haka grave. When he arrives at the station platform, the fields are blanketed with snow, which dampers all sound. The train blares its horn as it chugs away, and in the ensuing silence, he feels, impossibly, alone. He can make out his childhood home in the distance, the kitchen window, the potted succulents on the sill, sitting like orderly children queuing for sunlight. It hits him all over again that his mother will not be trooping down the steps to welcome him, that she will not be waiting as she always promised. They are both bad at keeping their word, aren't they? Maybe these things run in the family.

Neighbor Akari comes out to greet him instead. She has aged so much he barely recognizes her. He used to think she was so attractive, with her waist-length black hair and storm gray eyes. Her eyes are almost transparent now, and her hair sheared short. She can barely look him in the eye. She smiles at him, comforts him, but hardly looks at him. Himari forgave you, she says again and again. She always said, the babies look just like you!

Sora tries to walk past Kondo's Convenience without crying. He walks into the store the night after the tsuya wake, in a rage, his vision blurring as if underwater. He remembers trying to buy something but wakes the next morning with no memory at all, shit-faced and hungover. Aoi was right when she said the kids shouldn't come on this trip.

He had told Aoi he never wanted the kids to see this place. But she'd corrected him: It's not Kondo, she said. You never wanted the kids to see your mother.

Was she right? He can't bear to imagine Aoi's hard, condemning face, which bears too much resemblance to his mother's. There is so much of Nakamura Himari here—in the paper snowflakes pasted on the storefront window, the birdfeed on the porch, left outside even in winter. He loved his mother, he did, but only as he could bear her. Himari loved him too, she did, but only as she could bear him.

He stares at his draft, at his pale, contrived understanding of her. He tried not to show his true sentiments in the narrative, but it is there, underlying every word: the burden of what it means to be her son. If he is honest with himself, Sora always knew he couldn't come back, because once he did, he would never be able to leave again. Himari wanted him back in Kondo, forever, to take on the burden of a family legacy he never sought for himself. Like a moth stuck in a lamplight, fluttering the same worn circles until it runs out of air.

And she would've had him die here.

Himari always said she wanted more children, Akari tells him, on his final day. She was sad about her infertility. But she also said you were like having three children at once. You had so many personalities in you! It was like having a big family, on a budget. Akari laughs and laughs. You know, she was so happy to have you.

Sora thinks: His mother, too, had many personalities. She was kind, and single-minded, and thoughtful, and unyielding. And that is why he cannot write this fucking draft. Because he can't figure out who she was when she passed.

And he can't figure out where she left him.

As Himari lay dying, she thought of her son and his wasted, terrible dreams.
As Himari lay dying, she thought, your father would be ashamed of you.
As Himari lay dying, she thought, honor your ancestors, if not in life then in death.

As Himari lay dying, she thought, I forgive you. I forgive you of everything! The sun opened in glorious array, birdsong filtered through the treetops, the universe sang in exaltation—

~~*As Himari lay dying, she thought of nothing at all.*~~

The Garden in Eclipse

Paul Grindrod

The tomatoes and cucumbers still growing in the garden are liars. Despite the late-September date they continue flowering and setting fruit as though they have all summer ahead of them.

Perhaps they are taking their cues from the okra and tobacco, warmer-season southern crops that don't usually grow well this far north. These, too, continue to flourish, as oblivious to their dislocation as to the dusting of snow that appeared on the mountains during the most recent storm. The tobacco stands taller than I am. We grew it for its flowers; the slender, pink, trumpet-shaped blooms cluster at the top of the plant—well above the huge leaves—nearly impossible, now, to reach up and smell without bending the plant down towards us. We'll hang the sticky leaves to dry for a Native American friend. The okra has barely gotten started. Used to much longer, hotter days, only one plant survived, but now it is blossoming regularly and producing its slimy, gelatinous pods. The threat of a first frost that will surely do them in is already in the air, although the average date for killing cold is still a week past the equinox.

Better the tender annual vegetables should study the sunflowers and apples for advice on weather. The russeted apples, presagers of fall, are mostly ripe; those that haven't already fallen or been pecked at by birds, are ready to be picked after frost nips them once for sweetness. Sunflowers, buckwheat, and amaranth have all gone to seed and are quickly being picked clean by house finches, chickadees, and a bumper crop of goldfinches.

These seed-bearers most appeal to the native birds, but much of the garden was planted with one eye on attracting bird life. On any day you might still see hummingbirds squabbling over feeding rights at the tubular pastel flowers of a sunset hyssop or see any combination of American and lesser goldfinches, house finches, and chickadees all vying for pre-winter food on the pendant seed heads. House sparrows and a stout, particularly well-fed mourning dove—nearly the size of a city pigeon—patrol the ground underneath, gathering whatever edible pieces drop from above. As the plants have all met their reproductive imperatives and are dying or dying back to wait out the winter underground, birds are—or should be—laying on extra fat either to see them through the leaner times here or fuel them on migration.

One morning outside the large front window, I am startled by the appearance of a summer-bright goldfinch on the desiccated sunflowers. Well past the time when most goldfinches have traded their summer dress plumage for winter drab, this male doesn't seem to realize summer is about gone and another winter's exigencies upon us. Still as unreasonably and unseasonably colorful as the calendula blossoms dotting the yard—they responded to cooler temperatures and some fall rain with a glorious late re-blooming—the male goldfinch is as surprising as the tobacco out back.

Not all the birds are so complacent. A few afternoons later, a pair of scrub-jays takes turns visiting the last seed-bearing sunflower, a giant, pendulous-headed Tarahumara heirloom with white seeds. One bird will dash into the garden, perch for a moment to scan for the dog and cats, and then hang upside down from the drooping head to glean the seeds of this late bearer. As one leaves, the other returns, going through all the same procedures. Scrub-jays cache food, and we are forever finding whole peanuts from someone else's feeder stashed in unusual places in the yard. These two are doubtless stuffing sunflower seeds somewhere for protection against later shortages.

Then there is a sound, the first time so faint and unexpected it nearly escapes notice altogether. It comes again, the distant cross between a whoop and a gurgle, what one field guide calls a "rolling bugle," the otherworldly vocalization of migrating Sandhill cranes. Sometimes they fly so high they are impossible to spot, but this time, after scanning for several minutes, four cranes with their stretched necks and long trailing legs soar by, moving south along the foothills of the Wasatch Mountains.

Scanning for the cranes, several other flying forms catch my attention. A small formation of soaring and tumbling dark, large birds fly by—ravens judging from their antics—perhaps half a dozen or so. Shortly after the ravens pass, another large dark silhouette cuts across the clouds, solitary and proportioned differently than the ravens. A red-tailed hawk, its relatively long wings are tucked into a glide, its short tail half-fanned, heading south fast on a hard, downwind tack. Over the next half hour several more hawks go by on the same line, almost directly over the house.

My big day of cranes won't come for another couple of weeks. On a day in mid-November with unusually warm temperatures and all the snow disappeared from the foothills, the crane sound comes again, this time a flock of at least 30 wheeling over the eastern edge of the city. They flash in and out of sight as the low afternoon light catches their wings one moment and fades when they bank away, a disorganized flock, circling loosely and looking for thermal lift as they drift southward. Half an hour later we hear cranes again and a second, larger flock goes by to the west of us, formed into three straggling 'v' shapes and flapping south with more determination than the first group. From where I stand in the backyard, I would guess they are as far west as the interstate corridor or the Jordan River, possibly following it as a leading line to the next wetland where they'll stop and rest.

Although nothing in our little garden attracts these larger species into this tiny bit of habitat, not only the common urban yard species and the migrants overhead keep us in birds here. One evening, almost too dark to distinguish it at all, a small owl flew through the yard and perched briefly on the peak of the garage roof. Almost certainly a western screech owl, it only lingered a moment before taking off again on its nightly rounds.

One cold, snowy morning last spring a sharp-shinned hawk spent the better part of an hour plucking the feathers from and devouring some hapless little songbird. The hawk sat on the sticks of a brush pile left over from pruning the juniper bushes between our yard and the next, its plumage fluffed against the cold so that it looked almost as round as it was tall. By the time it left and I could try to identify the remains, most of the feathers had blown away and there wasn't enough left to tell what it was. Sharp-shins are not unusual winter visitors to urban feeders, but lately this fall we have been seeing at least one adult and one juvenile more regularly, suggesting the hunting is good in our tiny patch of landscape. When the real depths of winter descend on us, these, too, will likely leave for warmer places, but it is not impossible to see the occasional sharp-shin hanging around at any time of year.

One day last summer a strange series of bird sounds alerted us to the oddest bird sighting in the yard to date. Perched on the phone line between our yard and the neighbor's was a blunt, large headed, but comparatively small bird, luminescent blue on the back with shades of green on the wings and a red cap on the head. I called a friend who raised psittacines—parrots and their ilk—and described it, but she wasn't sure from my estimation of its size what it might be. It turned out to be a peach-faced lovebird, someone's escaped pet. It stayed around for several days and I hoped to get close enough to grab it, but the lovebird was enjoying its freedom and wanted no part of letting any human get too close to it. It disappeared after a while, and I know it couldn't have survived even the mildest of Utah winters.

Although the lovebird was clearly an exotic, seeing the recent changes in phenology in the garden, the timing of natural events over the last couple of years—the goldfinch that hadn't gone into eclipse at the fall equinox, flowers blooming in mid-November, the relative paucity of chickadees and dark-eyed juncos that usually take over and are the most noticeable yard birds for much of the winter—I have to wonder if these are merely the result of cyclically unpredictable weather patterns or the beginnings of long-term change brought on by warming climate. The naïve optimist might welcome lovebirds and Neotropical migrants that apparently never lose their breeding plumage. Certainly, I have enjoyed the extra weeks of produce and flowers from my garden.

Sadly, though, I fear we are living in a false paradise. With the warmth has come drought. This summer was the driest garden season in the years I've been growing here. Even rainwater harvesting couldn't keep up with the desiccating temperatures; there wasn't enough rain to harvest for most of the summer.

Finally, as I write this, Thanksgiving a few days away, most of the trees have lost their leaves. Temperatures remain well above normal during the day and barely dip below freezing at night. The gooseberry bush outside the window has gone as fiery gold and crimson as any Vermont sugar maple in miniature. Elsewhere in the valley people are seeing mountain birds, altitudinal migrants, showing up in parks, cemeteries, and at backyard feeders—red crossbills, Steller's jays, nuthatches, and mountain chickadees. We may get a winter, yet.

I haven't seen the goldfinches for several days, but with the garden in its winter eclipse and the flower stalks composted, there isn't much left for them to eat until we hang a feeder. Until then, I am happy enough with the occasional northern flicker grubbing in the leaf litter, the robins, house finches, and English sparrows that enliven the place and keep the hawks fed through the colder months.

Just as the garden and the gardener need fallow time, a season of rest, so my birdwatcher's eyes need relief from the intense colors of summer birds. There must be a reason they spend only part of the year in breeding plumage, perhaps the better to amaze their mates when that season comes around again. Like coming out of mourning, we'll wait for an appropriate period of time to pass and then get back into the garden ready to plant, and to be amazed again by the first improbably bright yellow goldfinch of the coming summer.

Summer Night

Matthew J. Spireng

Bed on the porch,
katydids calling,
scent of corn pollen
from the fields,
dark, dark,
katydids calling,
heat lightning
in clouds
to the north,
dark, dark,
katydids calling,
scent of corn pollen
from the fields,
headlights from a car
crossing the creek,
sound of its engine,
tires on the road,
dark, dark,
katydids calling,
scent of corn pollen
from the fields,
hoot of an owl,
katydids calling,
deer snorting
in the corn,
dark, dark,
katydids calling,
train whistle distant,
katydids calling,
katydids calling,
katydids calling,
katydids.

Butter Splash

Benjamin Guerette

Welcome to the audition. My name is Brad Lobster.

I'm kidding. It's Brad Kessler. But could you imagine?

So, first off, who's excited for Red Lobster's LobsterFest?

How excited?

No, how actually excited? Show me with your hands.

Yeah! Those are some excited hands. Those ones too. I love it!

Great. So, before we get to all of the moves—shell cracking, fork twirling, lemon squeezing—I need to see your Butter Splashes. It's the most important part of any Red Lobster commercial.

The butter needs to blast out of the ramekin in a perfect circle splash, completely enveloping the lobster in slow-motion. It needs to be so forceful that it Butter Splashes all of the butter out. All of it. Not a drop left. Like no butter left for even a second bite of EndlessLobster.

A question! Beautiful.

A ramekin is a little cup for sauce or butter or salad dressing.

Because it's not called a little cup. It's called a ramekin.

So make sure the butter goes everywhere. All over the table. All over the other food that may or may not need butter. All over your giant plastic Pepsi—not Coke—cup.

You're just that excited for that first bite of EndlessLobster, this week only, at Red Lobster!

Well no, it doesn't matter! The commercial viewer doesn't consider "consequences." And I don't love that you called it that.

No, it's fine.

So when you Butter Splash, the joy that you feel about LobsterFest needs to project through the backs of your hands. You need to smile with the backs of your hands as you Butter Splash.

If you don't actually love LobsterFest—it will show on the backs of your hands.

More questions. I love it!

Well yes, I guess in theory you'd have to ask your waiter for another ramekin of butter after every bite. But that's how good the EndlessLobster is—that you can't even think about "inconveniences." It's that exciting!

No. You wouldn't ever get tired of Butter Splashing the butter completely out of the ramekin. That thought wouldn't even enter your brain. C'mon.

Listen. The happiness that you need to project in this commercial goes beyond silly worries of where the butter might go or what the possible ramifications are for eating food without any concern for the people around you.

Guys. You're not getting it. I don't know why you're all so fixated on the idea of "pure mayhem." This is about projecting the joy and excitement of EndlessLobster through your hands. This is not about "acceptable human behavior."

No, it would not get on your date! For Pete's sake. It doesn't. It wouldn't. And even if it did, it would be part of the experience. LobsterFest is an adventure.

The commercial viewers love seeing Butter Splash! They do!

Yes, actually. Lots.

Yes I do have friends.

The Dead of Winter

Renee Agatep

How broken the bones of that house
peeping through floorboards like keyholes
waiting for her to come out
mouth agape, swaying lantern

Peeping through floorboards like keyholes
schoolhouse stands in misty distance
mouths agape, swaying like lanterns
fogging the air with cloudscapes

Schoolhouse stands in misty distance
rooting up the path's gravel crust
fogging the air with our cloudscapes
knuckles cracking like candy

Rooting up the path's gravel crust
gawking boots and missing mittens
knuckles cracking like rock candy
bells ring free in gloomy dusk

Gawking boots and missing mittens
out from a waving glass window
bells ring free into gloomy dusk
calling her name with no answer

Out from my waving glass window
I thought one day we will forget
calling her name with no answer
how many seasons were spent

I thought one day we would forget
how broken the bones of that house
and how many seasons were spent
waiting for her to come out.

Priorities

Kate Grace Smith

He's on the balcony, been there all day with the canopy at half-mast, squinting into yet another deadline. When I step outside to join him, he says I look 'good,' and gratification hits me warm as the sun licking our side of the building.

That's when he asks me if I've noticed the mold on our bathroom ceiling.

Of course I have, I noticed it when we first moved in last year, and I got up on a chair and painstakingly sponged off the spores. I noticed it again several months later, mentioned it in the hope he would take action, and when the hint dropped unnoticed, I scrubbed the ceiling once more.

Not long after, I saw the fungus sprouting up for a third time and decided to leave it.

In the kitchen, I put on a podcast about forgiveness and prepare lunch. Chopping board, pans, butter, and garlic. The cat curls around my feet, curious and hungry. Upstairs, the neighbours are dancing. I haven't danced in over a month.

Lamb might be traditional but it's pricier than we can afford right now. Who am I to buy eight lamb chops at a time like this? A quick glance at the clock tells me it's not a wholly unacceptable hour to start drinking.

He always tells me that the kitchen is my sanctuary, and I seem to get irritated if he disturbs me there when I'm cooking.

I don't even like cooking.

We sit down together, and I sense his red-rimmed, skittish mood straightaway. He knocks back the tumbler of wine in a few gulps before eating anything.

The lamb chops are overdone. Something close to shame washes over me. When he says nothing, he's making a point of being polite. Tough meat, lumpy potatoes, bland vegetables —a comically bad meal.

Jaw pistoning, he refills his glass. The evening slips by, malformed off-spring of the morning and afternoon, grown so close as to be indistinguishable.

I'm on the balcony watching her move down the street. I've learned her patterns, and I watch her return every time, my moonlit vigil.

At the apartment block opposite, she lifts the mask from her face, throws back her head, takes a deep breath of the crisp air. Then another, and one more—three luxurious inhalations.

I crane over the railings to catch a better glimpse, and she suddenly looks in my direction. Startled, I rear back, but she's perfectly still. Pale face, steady gaze; she could be smiling, but it's too dark to know for sure.

After a moment, she tilts her head and lifts one white gloved hand in greeting. Then she turns, unlocks the door, and goes inside.

(Poem on the eighth anniversary of his stillbirth)

J. Nishida

The eight-year-old with dark brown hair—
somewhere between my mouse and his father's jet—
and those eyes—is it the Asian chromosomes,
or something more?—
      isn't here.

His yells and giggles, this time of year,
chasing one of the cats with that
six-year-old—
          his sister
and partner in mischief—
the crash of the overturned chair,
or, God forbid, the falling
Christmas tree—the one they chose,
      too massive,
too top-heavy, and laden with a world
of dangling, fingered memories—
unpacked, unwrapped, and hung
      to reflect
for a time, upon the outstretched boughs—
            only to be lifted,
wrapped, and packed again—now a wild
tinkling in the air, a smash upon the ground—
      the groan
and yell of parents, as the two little ones stand—
      those small, bare feet—
amid the clamor, the shatter, a scattering of cats,

the pounding of our larger feet—
         as they gaze in

amazed horror, and growing astonishment,
at their own tiny might
              in this world—

      are not here.

Instead, peaceful sounds—the humming of
an only child, a sigh as she brushes back her long,
dark-chocolate-brown hair from those elegant eyes,
as she draws the figures from her imagination,
                    the tick of a clock
on my bedside table, the quiet scratch
of my pen as I write, examining all the
little shards—

      the weight of him,

      his warmth, yet from my womb,

      his sweet smell,

      and the stillness of him,

                    in my empty arms.

The Little Dog Laughed

Bruce Meyer

There was one day, and I don't know what got into him, but he called me into the spare bedroom upstairs and he was sitting on the floor. In his lap he had some books, children's books, and he was weeping and reading out a nursery rhyme to me.

"Hey diddle, diddle," he said sobbing and wiping his eyes on his shirt sleeve as he stared into the pages of that child's book.

I sat down beside him on the floor and did what I could to comfort him. After that, he kept the door to that room closed. There were pictures of clowns on the walls, and a shelf full of brightly coloured books. I never saw him that sad again.

Sometimes, when I knew he was feeling down, I'd do something stupid to make him laugh. I'd come into the room, pick up the first thing I could find and toss it in the air so it would come down and hit my butt. We'd laugh and laugh over dumb stuff like that. He used to say I had an infectious laugh because I'd throw back my head and roll my eyes and the more he laughed the more I would laugh. He'd cry then too, but it wasn't the same sort of crying I'd witnessed up in the closed front room.

He used to call me on hot summer nights to watch a ballgame on TV. He wasn't a fan of any particular team. He just loved the game. It would be hot as blazes in the house, hotter upstairs, because he would often say as he wiped his brow that he didn't believe in air conditioning. It made his joints ache.

The next day, we'd go out before breakfast for a game of catch in a vacant lot near the house and he'd replay the calls from the previous night, and when he'd say, "Here comes the pitch, it's a pop fly and the runners are going," I'd make a point of giving him a great catch. Sometimes, I'd even pretend there was a cut-off man and he'd have to run after it, but mostly I was good at fielding and he'd tell me how much he appreciated what I could do. He'd say I had a career in the majors waiting for me.

"My man," he'd say, "you'll be in the show in no time," and when we'd stop at the corner store for a quart of milk on the way home and the door would open I'd feel a whiff of cool air from inside. We'd go back to his place and sit in the kitchen while he drank his coffee. He'd offer me some, but I wasn't into it, but just for offering I'd remind him in little ways he was a good sport.

I needed to look after him. His wife had passed several years before, and he'd say, "Mack, you're all I've got. We'd better stick together."

If he was gardening, I'd hang out with him, help him dig the beds in the spring when he put in new plants, and when he cut the grass in the cool dusks of late summer I'd make sure he hadn't missed any patches. I don't think his eyesight was good. One night, I went ahead of the mower and just in the nick of time saved a small cedar waxwing that had fallen out of its nest. If I hadn't been there, he'd likely have run over it. We looked after the hatchling until it was big enough to fly around the living room, and one day we went out into the garden together and he let the bird go from his hands. It took off and flew into the trees and we never saw it again. That was a beautiful moment, just watching it go somewhere and not look back.

The mother must have thought it was dead. After the bird had fallen from its nest and we'd rescued it, she must have sensed it was still alive because she'd be up in her tree and scold us if we sat out in the evenings on the front porch. People would walk by and call to us. They always saw us together, and they'd call, "And how about you, Mack?" I could have told them I was fine. It was him I was worried about.

We had long discussions about growing old. Time is something everyone has to face. It is better to understand in advance than to have it arrive as a surprise. I never felt that old. I figured it was he who was slowing down and I was just keeping his pace so he wouldn't feel bad.

"You know," he said, "the worst thing that can happen to a guy is to die alone. People leave the room during the final moments because they are afraid of what they will see. I promise you this, if it ever comes down to it and you're at the end, I'm not going to leave you alone." I felt the same way about him.

But when the ambulance came for him after he'd grabbed his chest and fallen down the stairs, after the neighbours heard me calling for help at the top of my lungs for hours, the attendants wouldn't let me go with him. The guy next door invited me over to his place, but when I went out in the morning to stretch my legs in his yard I realized the garden wasn't gated.

The old guy had taught me where just about everything was in town—the post office, the druggist, the hardware store, the corner milk place, and the hospital. There was a woman coming out of the hospital—it wasn't as big as the hospitals that ask for donations in the commercials that interrupted our baseball games—and she had a baby in her arms and her husband was pushing her in a wheelchair. I would have stopped to say hello, but I felt an urgency to find him. I sensed he was in distress, that he wanted to see me, and that he was alone and afraid. I'm not sure how I knew, but I get very strong feelings and the feelings told me to take the elevator up to his room on the third floor.

I found him in a bed behind a curtain. He was hooked up to machines that made sucking sounds and beeped. I stood beside the rails and saw his eyelids fluttered open. He knew I would come. It was almost as if he was expecting me, that he had called to me, not in words but in thoughts. I wanted to tell him that I kept my part of the bargain, just as I knew he would have kept his had it been me and not him. He smiled. He was glad I was there, and I was glad that I was there too. I could feel it. It would have been terrible had he looked around and no one was there for him. There was a plastic clip on one of his fingers, but he reached out with his hand and stroked my head, and the last words he said were, "My Mack. Good dog."

Chores

Una Lomax-Emrick

Here in California, everything is green. That is not new. Even our old house, the one we rented with the scarred linoleum kitchen and the walls that smelled like fighting, had windows blocked off by sharp fallen leaves and ancient, patchy grass. Back then, my father worked long hours and kept secrets. At night, he'd retreat to the comfort of a private browser, of nudie flicks he swore were a thing of the past. During the day, he kept secret bags of potato chips in the back of his truck. My mother and I always heard them wrinkling, smelled the hidden salt and oil in the end. Back then, in that house with the scarred floor, my mother used to grieve. She used to call me on the phone and tell me that she was running out of people who would remember what it was like when she smoked cigarettes, in the days when her friends went to Simon and Garfunkel concerts and lost their shoes on the beach. She'd recount another set of relatives stone faced in the daylight service, drunk to hell that night. Her hair began to fall out, at first in little strands then in patches. She called me from the old house to tell me not to worry, that the world was just teaching her how to die.

Here, the air is salty but calm: it smells old with little notes of earth and the happy decay that comes with rain. Fog rolls in early and then drifts off the barn in cooked pasta tendrils of smoke. This house is in a glade, speckled with moss and decorated inside with white walls and bare planks of wood. We fall asleep to ocean sounds and wake up to quail noises on the little paths they make in the trees. Our walkways are weathered wood and packed dirt with pebbles; it was all here before us. My mom says that living here is healing her. My dad rises early and reads as the little winds move the trees by their bedroom. My parents walk for hours together and order beet and carrot seeds to the new mailbox. They invest in hearty boots and double layer work pants. They sit by the fire and laugh and wake up and argue over the breakfast table and the funny windows that trap our kitchen fumes. They are planning for years together, a new thought, a haphazard guarantee etched in the Lost Coast redwoods like the initials of young lovers.

Meanwhile, the dog keeps coming back from the backyard with deer ticks neatly attached to his belly. Under white fur, his skin is pink and smooth with little brown polka dots mapping a funny mutt's giraffe rug on his bald underarms and stomach. I hold his head in my lap and gently flip him onto his back, trying to dodge rogue teeth while making sure he doesn't flop on top of my dad's careful hands. We apply rubbing alcohol, my dad takes the silver tool that looks like two knives pressed together and pops the swollen tick out of his skin, then rushes its body to the bathroom for a more thorough extermination while I tell our dog that he has been a good boy. My mom sits perpendicular to the action, lips pursed. In the evenings, after walking miles along the narrow trails, she prompts us to check each other's hairlines. I search the crease under my mother's breasts and in her belly button, all out of her view after facts of gravity, my birth and scars from her surgeries that marked funny orbitals on her skin.

When I came back here, I thought that the staying would be temporary. My friends drove me to the Boston airport, the heavy March sun and humidity floating over narrow New England freeways. They helped drop my bags at the check in counter and hugged me goodbye with muted sadness. I shipped most of my possessions home a few days before my flight, a kettle wrapped in newspaper had already started winding its way back to my parents' house. My friends and I anticipated a reunion sooner than later: narrow hallways filling up with photos and a couple handles of cheap liquor on the bureau. The view from the airport was flat and light. I nodded my way through the Patriots flags, donned a mask, and sat back in my window seat. I slept for most of the flight and when the plane landed, I remembered again that California is as big and dark as you let it be. I spent the next two weeks in the attic, waiting to see if I was sick.

When I am worried, I like the feeling of warm water on the backs of my hands. After two days at home, I woke up with a sore throat and started to cough. I drove the lonely 10 miles up the big highway to the clinic and Barb, the town doctor, told me to keep everything clean. I was tested for COVID and returned to our attic with precise instructions to scrub my palms for 30 seconds and to stay out of the kitchen and the living room. The next day, my body felt well, but I was still worried. When I washed my hands, I began to balance my phone on the edge of the bathroom mirror and play sitcoms into the basin to time the rinsing. I scrutinized the faces on the little screen as I took the Dove sensitive bar soap from its silver dish and scrubbed as the seconds and minutes ticked by. The days I waited to know if I was infected were spent learning how to lose myself in the ringing of hands. Time passed easy that way, in tiny faces and coffee shop scenes. I faded into myself as my fingernails dug into the soap over and over, making their moon sliver patterns in the white molded glycerin

The results came back negative. I greeted my parents and began to unpack and cook. When the chores were done, I'd scrub the lengths of my hands and then up my forearms, close to the elbow. On good days, I could quickly cover in soap, rise, and leave but at other times, I washed and washed and exited the bathroom only to move to the kitchen sink or a dwindling supply of hand sanitizer in the pantry. I am still worried. Now, the warmth has become my favorite part of the day, the seeping, almost too-hot stream bubbling over skin, soothing it. Then I dry off, and the dog jumps up, scratching my forearms in his excitement, and I look down to see the red shavings of skin that his nails etch along my golden-haired wrists, my skin left dry and cracking from the soap and the faucet stream. The dog smiles up at me. I wash again.

Our yard is overrun by blue jays during the daytime and black speckled mosquito hawks at night. Today, I cut my hair on the shaky redwood flats out back and left the pile of thick golden pieces to clean up later. My mom watched as blue bird after blue bird swooped down to collect the straight blonde locks. They're nesting, so they like our dandelions and unmowed grass and the little pieces of hair that litter the deck near the trees. I don't sweep up the hair just yet, instead letting them thump their way through a part of my body that I've discarded and do not miss.

When I'm at home, I like bare feet. I walk on the wood and the gravel and cement of the barn floor. I cross hallways, vacuum and scrub with blue painted toenails chipping. I wash the soles of my feet at night, carefully noting new calluses and the funny peeling around the heel as I soap up in the little plastic shower. When the groceries and mail come, my father and I set them on a folding picnic table in the sunlight and spray each with 409 or a mix of bleach and water, wipe down and repeat until all of the threats are scrubbed away. My dad uses the paper towels sparingly and is done spraying and wiping in half the time it takes me. I change my clothes and wash my arms up to the elbow in the kitchen sink. After dinner, I clean plates by hand first, piling squirt after squirt of dish soap on our little sponges. I load them into our steely dishwasher and set it to sanitize. Then I walk upstairs, careful not to touch the railing, and am satisfied.

The attic is filled with spiderwebs. A few weeks ago, I removed the screens from the windows and was met by a very pale arachnid who clambered toward me with conviction, almost humming in his vengeful little way. I screamed and squashed him with the sole of a dirty sneaker. My best friend's least favorite part of killing bugs is cleaning them up after they are smashed. She once showed me the moth that was wiped, grey and chunky, across her lilac childhood walls. I don't mind the cleanup but hate the moment before when I have to breathe out and do the damn thing. When I was a child, I had a bad habit of closing my eyes right as the ball came towards me in softball and soccer and basketball. Parents would moan as I entered the goal wearing gloves and the orange kit, a guaranteed loss. There was a rule in peewee softball that they had to throw until the batter hit, and I would stand on home plate as the minutes ticked by, smiling at my parents who sat patiently and winced in the stands.

Coming home was the easy part. Now I'm here, trips out of bed take longer. There is always more to wipe down. I pour disinfectant on doorknobs and light switches and cabinet handles. I apply rubbing alcohol to the fingerprints on my iPhone. I spray the towel rack. Then I spray the counters and wipe them with a sponge. Then I scrub them with a toothbrush. My thin wrists and knuckles have begun to bleed now, they have a chalky pink hue from the bleach and the soap. I decide that my feet are too dirty, too hard; I shower earlier and vacuum the carpet on my hands and knees. I change sheets and flip pillowcases. I put too much detergent in the washing machine, and it won't drain properly. I stand next to it, pressing the same buttons over and over again. Soon, the backs of my knees are itching and red, rubbed raw with the hard water and soap residue dried into my jeans. I cover the couch in a blanket. I pump lavender lotion all over before bed, unwittingly slathering oil onto my phone screen. I clean it in the morning.

My mother passes through the kitchen and my dad pulls her in for a bear hug. He smiles, head resting on hers, and tells her that soon it will be warm enough to go into the ocean. They can't wait for the beaches and the sand and the winding paths through the flowers. The sun shines through the windows of the dining room, illuminating the two of them in the narrow door frame, golden and young. They go out again to the warmth through the trees. I go back upstairs and sleep.

The Confession

John Sibley Williams

Forgive me this small box of synonyms
                     borrowed from older tongues.

& forget the telephone game we played last night
             when only my voice carried, intact.

That there are no rules to it all, just instinct & mistranslation & loving
            our slice of the world, by which I mean where *trespass*

confuses with *own*. That none of the bones the river coughs up
          are mine. Never mind that heights are measured in hands & distance

by the chasm between hand & reached-for star. There's no room for stars here.
No barbed fence someone hasn't raked herself over so her son can live

that much closer to hope, shelter. Forgive me the bullet
      a stranger lodged in your language, that when I say *the body*

I mean it abstractly. Show me the heart a mother must eat so her son
       won't suffer our tomorrows. Plant it in my hands. Let's agree

something should grow there. Let's pass *should* around this circle of ears
      & mouths & see if it changes in the end. Never mind

that it always changes in the end. Forgive me the stars I don't have to reach for.
            These bones that still aren't mine. & the box. This small box.

The Near Occasion of Sin

William L. Alton

Every October, the church put on a festival. They had a dinner. Handmade sausage and kraut. No beer. Gethsemane Baptist had no tolerance for alcohol. They had carnival games. A cake walk. Bobbing for apples. Ring toss. They filled a pool with rubber ducks and gave out live goldfish as prizes. Most of which died in their little plastic bags before getting to the car. There was music but no dancing. Gethsemane Baptist had no tolerance for dancing. Dancing was sexual and sex was bad, except if you were married. And, sometimes, even then.

Old women, widows, like Aunt Faye, and the bitter wives of men who spend most of their evenings at the VFW worked the booths. Starched and proper. Dressed in modest gingham and linen. Broad hipped and ironically bosomed. They herded the crowd and served the food. They passed out the treats with small scraps of Scripture tied them. Also, they watched with cruel eyes for any sign of chicanery or foolishness.

It was Halloween week. Getting cold. Wet. Clouds snagged on the mountains like wool dragged out in raw strings. The wind gnawed at people's faces. Sullen kids stumbled through the festival with their families. Any festival was better than no festival. People in Izard lived simple lives. Small excitements grew large here.

In Izard, Halloween was a quiet night. Gethsemane Baptist had no use for Halloween. No use for masks or extortion. "The pagans," Pastor Foster said. "Wander the world. They look to lead you into sin." People listened to Pastor Foster. Sin, in Izard, was a real thing. Quiet though. Done privately. We kept our iniquities in our closets. Behind closed doors and locked windows. At the festival, no one wore costumes. No one tricked. No one treated.

People put on their church faces. Smiles empty of joy. Eyes flickering like bats. They listened for gossip's snicker. The near occasion of sin.

The Original Baa Baa Dude

Cal LaFountain

With winter fading, spring freshified the land. Every cell of life on that farm beamed a vibrant howl and the first of the baby goats were born. I discovered two of them one morning in the field beside mothers browsing the foliage. Their noobie jawlines pumped in mimicry of the herd's elders.

An indent in the grass pillowed the third kid. I tapped it with my boot and a swarm of flesh-flies dispersed in a flash of rotten air. The overnight moisture shaped dewy mohawks on its rump.

Wilton peeled the corpse from the spongy earth. He carried it to the electric fence on the hillside and tossed it over. Men like Wilton maintained the chain of agriculture, men who performed the ugly tasks without hesitation.

In winter's absence the kids multiplied. They flicked and wiggled their tails. They hopped around the fields and birth pens as together they learned to use their bodies. Wagers teetered between us about which mother might pop next, as many threatened, their plump udders and swaying teats in evidence of ripe birth terms.

Though through April a general warmth sustained the days, one unlucky kid dropped from his mother overnight in a fluke surge of freezing temperatures. Junie found him shivering blind beneath a membrane of afterbirth slime, separated from the cold-shield safety of the herd, his survival fraught in ill-favor. He was the official runt outcast of the herd. Because his mother rejected his attempts to feed, Hadley and I adopted him and fed him three times every day with a powdered milk solution. We named him The Original Baa-Baa Dude.

The fields' jutting rocks served as the testing grounds for the kids' motor skills. One rock in particular held status among the group for its steep edges. Juvenile skirmishes littered its base and day after day, the kids flopped from its peak.

For weeks The Original Baa-Baa Dude bobbed around alone at the rock's periphery, timid to engage with the others. Then one day he mustered the gumption to join. But he lunged too fast and crashed headfirst into the rock. The largest kid was the first of the hierarchy to drift from him. The rest of the group then joined as they abandoned their preferred spot to scan the field for new playgrounds.

In the birth pens, while pitchforking the afterbirth sacs of a recent birth, replenishing hay, and fanning diatomaceous earth, Junie told Hadley and me about the time she had left Greeneville for a weekend in Nashville a few years back. "When I got home," she said, "Wilton told me one of our bottle babies had died overnight. He said it was too weak to feed itself right." She bent low to extract from the haybed a pungent cluster of goat turds she called 'nanny berries' and whispered. "I can't prove it, but I'm sure he snapped its neck."

Every morning we used a soda bottle to mix The Original Baa-Baa Dude's meals. Once the ratio was right, we capped the bottle with a rubber feeding nipple and held it under hot water until it warmed. We cut up some old socks and wrapped them around the bottle to hold the temperature as we walked the fields to find him.

The rest of the kids fed with enthusiasm, butting at their mothers' udders for withheld stores of milk. The Original Baa-Baa Dude had his own way of charging at the bottle whenever we fed him, but his spitfire blitzes always landed him past the rubber nipple. When the milk solution was gone, he would charge the bottle a few more times until we pulled it away. He'd lie a few minutes in one of our laps, a faux milk foam ringing his mouth, cuddling up with snout puffs and a warm steady heartbeat. When we left for other chores, we watched as he trailed the herd alone, awkward and uncanny, in obvious contrast to the consensus bounce of the other kids. A few times he noticed us watching him and turned back, tried to angle a jump through the electric fence, got shocked, and bleated his high squeal out over the property.

The fields' electric fences likened the boundary of my life's direction; so many possible paths and causes in equal weight; it splayed shin-bonkable obstacles and covert damage volts, infinite offerings empty of any proof for their legitimacy as correct, or incorrect courses of action. I had no idea what I should do, and I shared this shortcoming with The Original Baa-Baa Dude.

Among our justifications for the runt's defects, the powdered milk solution surfaced. We thought it might lack the ruminant nutrient profile that helped bind the herd on a shared social ground. Whatever the explanation, some essential quality of The Original Baa-Baa Dude was Off, something never activated, features not installed, a goat-housed switch not flipped, or one never present with the option of On.

Lying together in bed one night, Hadley and I watched "BAM" by M+A. We watched grimy violent footage of the Pistons-Pacers brawl of

2004. We watched *Manhatta* by Paul Strand. We watched a video of the Dorrie level from *Mario 64* on mute, while in a separate tab we played "Rhubarb" by Aphex Twin. We watched *Buffalo '66*. We kissed. The World's Squeakiest Mattress squeaked.

"There's something really wrong," Hadley said. "With the runt. He's always running past the bottle and falling down. Plus his little baa-baas sound all hoarse and scratchy and wrong. He doesn't sound like the rest of them. He doesn't even sound like a goat. It hurts me that his mom won't feed him. The other ones won't play with him. There's something really wrong with him." She was right. There was something really wrong with that little goat, but we made him ours.

Winchester

Mayneatha Royal

Winchester
One block from Damen
Two blocks from the street my high school crush
Was shot down on

Winchester
One block from Wolcott
Two blocks from the alley where my homie Devonte
Was killed by the Chicago police department

Winchester
Three blocks from Wood
Four blocks from the school Kevin and I attended
Until the night he was killed
At a party that I was invited
But wasn't recommended to go to

Winchester
Six blocks from Marshfield
Six blocks from the alley where twelve-year-old Jahmeshia
Was found raped
Beaten
And unresponsive
We went to the same grammar school

Now it's mid-July
90 degrees
No summer breeze
No windchimes
You see the block's kinda quiet today
But I don't say this with pride
Because silence is deadly
Somebody's always watching

Yeah
My block may be lowkey
But it's never empty
You see
Winchester taught me to watch my mouth
To analyze my homies
Cause the one who say they got yo back
Could be the same
With a nine to yo spine
Ready to end your life over
Five dollas
Two quarters
Three nickels
And a dime
Show no love
Never get caught lacking
Show no sympathy
That's three laws in these streets
So lock your doors
And barbwire your windows
Cause today is the block party on 64th

I don't advise you to come to the block party on my street
You see
Nightmare
is loose and looking for a game to play
But I wanna know who lets a FULL GROWN pitbull
out loose on
the block
in the middle of the day anyway

Kids please don't come to the block party on this street
Cause Mr. Percy's preaching the gospel
But holding hands with little Bobby
While Ms. Harrison's asleep

Ma'am please don't leave your home for this block party
Darnell's sneaking through Ms. Fenley's backyard right now

Cause you know
Unprotected possessions are easy money
To a petty thief

Young men no need to come to the block party on my street
Insanes are on the next block
And I hear D-ville was coming up the street
I'm not playin no games
Or talkin about Labron James
When I say these young brothas are bringing nothing but the heat
And you can take it
Or leave it
It's just a little advice
Coming from a young girl
Living in the belly of the beast
Mid-July
Summertime
Winchester
Isn't the place to be

Fiction First Prize

Proxy

James D'Angelo

At dawn the American guns open up and vent Hell's exhaust.

The shells rain until dusk falls, always on faraway places.

They do this every day.

At night, sharpshooters with Starlight scopes command the sight lines. They can spot the cherry of a cigarette from nine hundred yards and kill the man smoking it before the nicotine reaches his lungs. The snipers were American when the war started, but now most are local militia we've been training. One of these locals told me he'd killed at least five men "the cigarette way."

The U.S. military has spent countless research dollars to make soldiers more effective. They found that the mechanical distance between killer and victim is a key factor in willingness.

Imagine strangling a child.

Skin to skin.

The distance is zero.

You can stop.

Unless you're a serial killer, that was probably hard to stomach. But now imagine loading a shell into a long metal tube. Imagine calculating windage and elevation. Imagine pulling a lever. Is this easier? The distance is now ten miles or more, but it will kill more children than your hands ever could.

Firing artillery. Shooting at the tips of cigarettes. It's easy to lose track of cause and effect.

Everyone has code names because none of us are supposed to be here. Because the war isn't really happening. The soldiers are anonymous, from places you couldn't find on a map. Places like Sun City, Kansas, or Muddy Gap, Wyoming.

Major Ringo commands the guns in the town dubbed Jericho. The rest of the Beatles are deployed to the south and west. Ringo calls me Magpie and disguised me as a translator. "It's fine if you don't speak the language," he said. "We're not here to negotiate."

He also doesn't let me look like a journalist. No press badge, notebooks, or tape recorders. He's permitted me one disposable camera, but to protect his men, the photographs can't include faces.

The story will only be what my memory and camera can hold. One photo shows the local sniper silhouetted against the moonlight. Like all the militia, he sports a new uniform and a clean haircut so he looks official when the war is won. Another snapshot depicts the machinery of death that keeps time. It's impossible to miss the words US ARMY stamped on the 155-millimeter barrel. My third picture is a prisoner's portrait. He's a suspected saboteur held in the town's jail. Chained to the wall, he wears a black hood over his head.

The man in charge of the prison greeted me with a yellow-toothed smile. He wore a ragged scarf around his neck and carried his pistol tucked into his pants.

"You're a journalist," he said immediately.

"What makes you think that?"

"Unlike you Americans, I'm not very busy. So I notice things." He motioned me into a side hallway, desperate to talk. "Before the revolution, I was a medical student in Boston."

"Why'd you come back?"

"I came home," he said. "My father is dead. I'm the oldest son. My brother's only sixteen. What else could I do?"

Before he led me to the cells, he begged me to take his photo. He said his father would've been proud to see him in uniform. Then he told me a joke but I didn't laugh.

"Maybe I translated it wrong," he said. "It's really funny."

The prisoner screamed for water in broken English and the militia men guarding him shared rumors that the enemy tortures their prisoners.

"Maybe we do the same," one said. "Start with the pliers."

"We should shoot him," the other said. "Filthy traitor."

From the outside it has to appear that final victory came from people like this, so U.S. intelligence started rumors to help stretch the moral distance between rebels and regime. Men who torture prisoners are evil, and killing bad guys is so easy, even kids' movies do it.

Major Ringo meets me in the lobby bar of the hotel that's still hosting dignitaries and courageous adventure tourists. He trades me information for cigars and bourbon. He talks until the bourbon's gone or he gets bored.

That's our deal.

"The front's closing in," he tells me. "You have to leave."

"So we're losing?"

"Losing's our job, Magpie. Stretch the enemy thin, pull them out of position. Other battalions swoop in for the kill."

"How long?"

He puffs and downs the bourbon in one swallow. A tap on the glass means the answer will cost me another drink. The waiter barely speaks English, but has learned to bring two glasses, just in case.

"So, how long?"

"Two days at most. We're moving fast. Every enemy can adapt." He bends back to take in the hotel's sparse guests that he's responsible for evacuating once Jericho falls. The waiter rests on the bar, chatting with its gruff owner. Farther on, a woman mops the tile floor. Farther still are two men in suits who were part of the local government council and think that still matters. A boy no older than ten plunks a coin into the jukebox and a scratchy jazz melody plays.

When I have free time, I talk to the residents if I can get beyond the language barrier. Most of them were happy for American help at first, but the welcome's wearing out. They want an end to war, and the Americans gone.

Ringo's craggy hand strokes thick stubble. Soldiers are meant to stay clean-shaven, he told me once. There are some psychological benefits to maintaining a daily routine and not letting war turn you into an animal. But once you gut a man with a bayonet, you're most of the way there.

"Where's the battalion headed next?"

"That's classified."

In war, words take on new meanings. Every meeting with Ringo is another lesson, and the first time we talked, I learned that classified means he can't tell me without implicating himself.

"Where *are* we winning? Maybe that's where the story is."

The drinks arrive and he sips. "No need for insults. We both want this war exposed."

"Then get me some action. Something to end it."

"If things get too hot, it's prison for me. You win a Pulitzer."

"This isn't about a medal."

"So what's it about?" he asks.

"Haven't you had enough war? Why'd you contact me if you haven't?"

"I have. But you're never done with it." He pauses, inhales. "You remind me of my son, actually. The way you won't quit."

"Is that why you're helping me?"

He says nothing for a while, only gulps the bourbon and examines his stained uniform. Between his ragged beard and wrinkled cap are tired eyes. Eyes that say he's been at the zero distance and clawed his way back.

"No," he says at last. "I've seen your work. You believe in what you're doing. Now, if you want some action, that can be arranged."

"Why now?"

He leans in, blows smoke into my face. "The chain of command's getting rusty. Don't ask why. You'll have your story." He slides me the last glass. "And you'll need a drink where we're going."

The guns roar outside, signaling another day. Sunlight billows through the revolving doors.

Speaking above the tantrum is impossible. He motions for me to follow across the street to a bank where the command center is nestled in the underground vault. The bunker's thick walls barely mute the concussion. Between volleys, I ask, "How old's your son?"

"He was twenty-two."

Back home, the view is from ten thousand feet above, and you can't see through the clouds. This is the gist of what people believe:

The war hasn't been happening for three months. American advisors haven't been stationed here for two years. One hundred and fifteen American soldiers haven't been killed. Another three hundred and sixty haven't been wounded. We haven't been supplying guns and missiles to the rebels. We're sanctioning the regime because it's oppressive, and we support the rebels because they're fighting to bring democracy to their people.

War has made the definition of democracy unrecognizable. It's buried by saccharine headlines and deceptive speeches to the United Nations, but with enough grit you can dig through to the bottom and find the truth. You'll find no mention of free elections, or the will of the people. Here, the democratic side is the one who will provide a good home for our investment capital.

Government forces still occupy most of the territory. But the Major assures me that with the addition of American combat units, the rebels will win quickly. The people here are simple and tribal, he says. Once the regime falls, they'll bow to the new king of the hill.

Below the surface, in Major Ringo's office, he stabs his finger at a map pinned to the wall. "Here's where we are. Take a photo of this."

"I already know where we are."

"We're going here." He pokes another dot, maybe six inches away. It doesn't have a fancy code name, just the label V16. Somewhere between V16 and Jericho is a line of red pencil that signifies the front. It's been erased and redrawn many times.

"Our bombers were up to no good last night," he says. "It's an hour by chopper."

I aim the camera and wait for him to step aside before snapping the photo. "What's there?"

"Enemy territory." He digs under his desk and offers me a Kevlar vest. It slips on easily enough, but its weight is crushing. Headlines about my capture and public execution flash through my mind. And how they'll spin it to shift public opinion in favor of the war. When I recover, Ringo's handing me a pistol, grip first.

"In case we get overrun."

"Is that likely?" I ask.

"Colt 1911," he says. "Don't let the name fool you. It's only got seven rounds."

"I'm a terrible shot."

"You don't want to be taken alive. And you can't miss your own head."

The chopper dusts off and the pilot might be drunk but he's the only one on duty. "Are you a reporter?" he asks.

"Translator. But I'm on break."

"When you get off, tell me how to say fight your own fuckin' war!"

I nod and clamp my headphones tighter. We fly over the Devil's work. The landscape stretches on and on. Rocks loom over crumbling towns. Craters and skeletons of tanks are the only other features. Trees turned to charcoal long ago, and the clouds of grime never clear.

At some point, we cross the red pencil line, but you can't see it from up here. It's too small.

We land on a ridge where the grass smolders and ashes drift gently as snow in the chopper's vortex. Ringo leads me into the devastation. The air burns my eyes and sears my lungs and he hands me a rag to breathe through.

"White phosphorous," he says. "You never get used to it."

"Is it safe?"

"Don't get wobbly now." He forges ahead to where the ridge opens up and a wooden village is in shreds. Bodies stick to every surface. They line the dirt path. They hang out of windows. They're scattered in all directions, and from high above, probably look like fireworks frozen mid burst.

There's a man in loose black pants and no shirt. His skin is boiled in some places, bubbling up into yellow goop. In others it's peeled away, exposing raw muscle. Only a handful of hair remains.

"I'll need photos to prove it."

"That's why we're here, Magpie. Get the faces."

I snap the picture and move on to another body. Her clothes are cinder, her face stripped back to the bone in spots. Her mouth is closed, but teeth glimmer through fleshy holes. What's left of her eyes are shocked open.

"They're civilians?"

The Major keeps his distance, lights a cigar and looks away. "Intel said the enemy had a listening post here."

"Did they?"

"Three EKIA."

"And the rest?"

"Nobody counted."

"But why all this?" I ask.

"Overkill breaks the spirit. Forces surrender."

I capture the woman's image and fight my way through the rubble into a house's remains. The air inside is thicker and my eyes want to close but I force them open and make them witness. Two men in charred uniforms slump against wooden walls. From the right angle and distance, they'll both fit in one photo. One clutches his rifle with fingers that could pass for barbecued ribs. The other's pose resembles a drunken blackout and he could wake any second. His face is dirtied with soot and foam has pooled around his swollen lips and nose. He's died of inhalation and the real damage is on the inside.

On the outside, he's only separated from the rebels by the scraps of clothes he wears.

The final distance to put between killer and victim is cultural, but all the chemical agents in the world can't burn off the truth. In civil war, your enemy is yourself. This is the real reason we're here. No matter how small the space between, hired killers will squeeze in for the right price.

The chopper blades die out. Ringo's voice pierces the wind and I stand at attention for another lesson.

"Now," he says, "you know what winning means."

Notes From the Editors on "Orange is the Darkest Color"

Cadence Mandybura

Dear ████████████,

Thank you for submitting *Orange is the Darkest Color* to Ersatz Press for publication. While we have ultimately decided against accepting your novel, your work provoked great discussion among our editorial team. We've collected our feedback below.

> The writer has a fine premise here—what if a billionaire reality star became President?—as well as inventive details, such as vandalizing an official weather map, rambling about the yachting life to Boy Scouts, and abandoning an umbrella he couldn't bother to close. Where this story falters is in its abundance: it feels like a piling-on of the ridiculous, grotesque, petty, and, frankly, racist. This is exhausting for the reader. I advise the writer to pare this novel down to its most evocative details to give the readers more breathing room. —*S.D.*

> The tone of this novel is wildly inconsistent. Often the story is told with palpable realism—and good job there, your writing is certainly capable—but then a ridiculous event (a porn star, really?) will shatter the illusion. Further, the tone sometimes turns uncomfortably dark (e.g., migrant children in cages) with no satisfactory conclusion or payoff. I suggest you consider what you want this story to be—a comic romp, a cautionary tale, a character study, etc.—and reframe the novel accordingly. —*T.O.*

> I personally loved this novel: a surreal black comedy with the stakes of truth vs fiction winding higher and higher. Throwing in a worldwide pandemic is a daring, hyperbolic choice. Unfortunately, this edgy, dialed-to-eleven humor simply isn't a good fit for our press and readership. You may have more luck with niche presses such as Goblin Toes Publishing

or Whither Wither Books. This idea also has the potential for an episodic series, if you're interested in shifting the format to television. Good luck! —*M.M.*

You've quite brilliantly interplayed accusations of sexual assault (and admissions thereof) with a fictional social movement that holds predators to account. However, this was the most disappointing part of the book to me: very little real change occurs, and your president gets away scot-free in spite of his deplorable behavior. What message are you trying to convey to your readers, especially girls and women? —*S.P.*

Please remember that feedback on works of fiction is always, to some extent, subjective. We hope these notes prove useful and encourage you to keep writing.

Sincerely,
The Editors

No Sanctuary
(Seminole Canyon, Texas)

J. Brent Crosson

"The cliff walls of Seminole Canyon preserve the documentation
of those who have made the journey for thousands of years . . .
—Enrique Gómez, "Of Hummingbirds and Immigrants"

It was the spring that the sky
was a blue cloudless shield,
a curved shelter
to protect against meteors.

It was the spring that the president
unveiled the family shield
of the new Space Force
to protect against space,
but refused to wear a mask
while touring a mask factory.

It was the spring that an asteroid
gave us a near miss,
the spring of the virus
that was a cold
war plot,
the president and his opponent
both assured us.

It was the spring of the wall,
of the social distance
that my cousin found in a state wilderness,
after a night of torrential showers
of rain, hail, and meteors
turned the dried-out creek bed
into a shallow scar of water
he'd lain down in.

The morning sun silvered
the wicker of the creek's rapids,
braids that ran over his chest and around pink rocks,
as hikers peered over the trail's edge,
in amusement or concern at his bathing spot.
But no one came close enough

to disturb the dragon fly
perched on the new earth
of his knee-cap—
a bone dome rising
above primordial waters
whose song,
like a long gargle that never stops for breath,
will be gone tomorrow
when some apocalypse
of summer will burn the canyon dry.

And my
cousin will be in cold storage,
in a cell of ice
and a.c.,
another casualty of this country's
unmasking.

Fangland

Alexis Wolfe

In the dying embers of the year, nearing the first anniversary of my son's vampire obsession, it happened. Stan suddenly began bleeding from the mouth, although he hadn't bitten anyone.

It was December 14th when the bleeding started. It was also Wear Your Christmas Jumper to School Day. Stan wore one featuring an upside-down Santa—legs and feet sticking up from a chimney—under his open coat as we waited outside for the doctor's surgery to open. He'd woken to find his whole body speckled with tiny red dots and circles of blood on his pillow, some fresh, some faded, overlapping like Venn diagrams.

The dawn sky seemed unusual, ablaze with pink and orange streaks. Our breath made clouds, conjoining in the cold air. Stan leaned on his long white cane, chin resting on his clasped hands. I dabbed the red droplets forming steadily on his lip with tissue. Right then, I still thought he'd be back at school by lunchtime.

Stan's vampire obsession had ignited back in spring, watching the movie Hotel Transylvania. Months had passed since he'd retrieved the old vampire cape from the dressing up box. He labelled that short, frayed swirl of polyester his Spring/Summer cape and later christened a new long cloak Autumn/Winter. He'd stopped asking to wear capes in public because my answer was always no.

After a black paint job, a doll's house was now the Dracula House, cardboard bats dangling from its ceiling. We were just back from Transylvania, the only thirteenth birthday present he'd requested. We'd travelled across Romania in a weekend, stopping to see Vlad the Impaler's fortress and Bran Castle where, at dusk, we stood and stared at clouds of bats. They were swooping and circling and perhaps Stan saw them or maybe he just pretended he did. He does that sometimes.

Other people joined the surgery queue and politely tried not to look. What a sight: a dishevelled mother, hair scraped hastily into a ponytail and the boy with the white cane and hearing aid, bloody mouth, and Christmas jumper. By the time the doctor referred us to the hospital, droplets of blood had landed on the yellow letters on his jumper, staining the double R's in Merry.

"You've just ruined my Christmas!" said Stan, hearing a blood test was imminent.

The doctor smiled at me.

"Don't be silly," I told Stan.

I resigned myself to a day of anxiety. The slow drip from his bottom gum was just the beginning; before long, red crusts were forming at the ends of his nostrils. On reaching the hospital, all his teeth—which stand like misaligned tombstones facing various directions in a badly designed graveyard—were streaked bright red. Blisters appeared inside his cheek and oozed more blood.

At first, I didn't see the connection. But when I messaged to say *We're in hospital, Stan is bleeding from the mouth*, my brother texted back immediately. *Oh no, poor Stan! PS. Have you checked for fangs?*

Stan smiled admiringly at his reflection in the hospital mirror. Today's look was more impressive than Halloween.

"Mum, I might be getting my fangs!"

I tied a white tissue pad around his neck like a bib, although we agreed to call it a cape. After thirty minutes, it was splattered like one of those psychological tests where you interpret the ink blots. Several cape changes later, it became obvious we'd be staying overnight.

The doctor's comment came that evening, after Stan transferred to the children's ward. "Did you not think to go to the GP sooner?" she asked, scribbling down that the rash first appeared two days before.

This took me by surprise. I considered myself consistently on top of Stan's health concerns, managing daily tube feeds, hearing aids, eye drops, and medications. Not to mention school communications, homework, his Education & Health Care Plan, a diary of outpatient appointments, and his general quirky behaviour.

I shook my head. Two days ago, I'd seen only a small red blotch, the size of a ten pence piece. Stan didn't have a fever or seem unwell. But still her words smarted. Had I been neglectful? My voice sounded defensive. "Besides, no one acted like this was an emergency. They said come in at 2 pm. It's taken all day to get this far and nothing has actually happened yet."

"Well, not nothing!" she corrected me sharply. "We've done a blood test, discovered his low platelets and will start him on steroids now."

We stared at each other for a moment. I felt myself stepping back into an old arena where the doctors' superior knowledge of medicine battled fiercely against my expertise with Stanley.

The doctor advised Stan's platelet count was 8, when it should be at least 150. Rather than vampiric transformation, she suspected ITP, where very low platelets lead to bruising and spontaneous bleeding.

Despite being put in my place, I felt lighter. At last, an indication they had a plan. I breathed out; maybe I could surrender, stop being in charge for a while. I wished my husband was here, but someone needed to be at home for Stan's brothers.

A cuppa would calm my nerves. Just beyond our cubical curtains, a baby grizzled relentlessly. Alongside regular baby murmurs, she made sounds particular to a baby with a nasal gastric tube: a certain wet gurgling cough, which I'd not heard since Stan had his nasal gastric tube removed at nine months. This forgotten soundtrack hurled me backwards in time.

Anxious about leaving Stan too long, I marched quickly, past the white Christmas tree with blue neon lanterns that stood sentry at our bay and into the main corridor of the ward. Nurses clustered around Reception, one with tinsel adorning her ponytail. I heard fragments of conversation about presents as I strode by. Pushing double doors with Santa stickers on their glass panes, I thought *He has to get out before Christmas. Christmas cannot be cancelled.*

Stan was confounding me again. My mistake was thinking I had him all worked out, his quirks understood. Priding myself on knowing exactly how he'd react in any situation. Now he was baffling me again, just as he did when he was born.

Back then he had shown up with an unexpected list of problems, X, Y and Z. As the consultant and his entourage lined up along the wall like an identity parade and begin to relay his issues, I remember feeling surprised the doctor had no notes. How could anyone memorise such a long list? Vision, hearing, heart defects, hormones, unsafe swallowing, and more. Stan spent seven weeks in hospital. Fifty-one excruciating days.

But I'd had two more children since then and although Stan had undergone ten operations and his outpatient appointments were still frequent, he had always been well. There'd been no hospital overnights since he was a baby.

In the Parent's Kitchen, several large sterilizing tubs stood on the counter. Seeing dismantled breast pump parts floating in these watery wombs, my stomach lurched. I remembered another hospital, a tub inscribed with my name. Lifting the wet pieces in and out, three-hourly for forty-five-minute milk expressing/torture sessions. The despair surrounding Stan's birth was not something I wanted to re-visit. *He'll be fine. Make a cuppa and get out of here.*

That evening, the cubicle bays were dimly lit from bedtime hour. Overhead lights left on inside storerooms reflected triangular shafts of light on the floor of the main corridor through the ward. Walking barefoot, my feet made tiny squeaks with each step. A brown, plastic, squirrel-shaped bin looked menacing in half-light, its gaping mouth a dark void below unblinking goggle eyes.

It was never silent on the ward; passing by other bays I heard low moans and groans, coughing or babies crying, and a nurse clattered around a blood pressure monitor mounted on a wheeled stand. Machines bleeped and alarmed as oxygen levels fell or drips were completed.

After midnight, a nurse sat nearby using a spare bed as a desk. Ting! Ting! She repeatedly snapped the metal springs of a ring-bound file, loud enough to puncture each thought. In the ward's stillness, with little soft furnishings to muffle, this noise echoed sharp as gunfire. Snap! Snap! Shuffle, Snap! I sat up in bed and rummaged around for the break in Stan's wall of curtains, tore it open with a flourish and glared at her, not caring how stroppy she thought I was. The noise stopped.

Over the following days I lost count of the blood draws.

"I'm sorry but you aren't very good at this!" Stan told a junior doctor, who'd failed twice to find a vein and was manipulating the needle inside his arm like a metal detector.

On the ward, time is magnified. Stan lay on crumpled white sheets, humming and swishing his iPad whilst blood dribbled slowly from his lips. He barely noticed, delighted he had discovered Hotel Transylvania 2 on the bedside TV. He found a strategy for blood tests, squeezing my hand hard to share the pain, his nails leaving half-moon-shaped indentations in my palm.

The doctors disturbed our tranquillity to contradict each other. Steroids were stopped and antibiotics started. The next day different doctors came, spoke amongst themselves, heads turning left and right like a parliament of owls. Antibiotics stopped, steroids resumed. IV infusions followed, first immunoglobulin and later platelets. For me, these were days spent blotting, wiping, coaxing dried clots off his lips with pink mouth-care sponges on little white canes. The blood got everywhere, crescents of it under my nails when I washed my hands. Months later I would notice tiny brown flecks on the page edges of *Olive Kitteridge,* the novel I read at his bedside.

Sometimes as Stan slept, I listened to his breathing, a gentle snore, and watched the mound under his blanket rise and fall. But mostly, I interrogated myself. Did I notice the rash earlier and ignore it? Or infect him with sloppy sloppy hygiene at home? Was I too relaxed about his health? Later, I learnt ITP is an autoimmune disease, and no one's fault.

On December 19th, we waited to be discharged. The bleeding had almost stopped, but his platelets might take months to return to normal. Stan finally tired of Hotel Transylvania 2 on repeat, repeat, repeat, and chose Christmas crafts. He half-heartedly stuck glitter, stickers, and fluffy balls on a cardboard cracker shape. The balls fell off. Next up, a festive crossword with his own alternative choice of words: vampire, stake, fangs, blood.

Then the waiting ended. A nurse handed over his medications and permission to leave.

"Stanley, you've been a real trooper!"

"Yes!" he said, completely mishearing her, "I'm a real true vampire!"

Home was exactly as I left it five days before. Unwritten Christmas cards and teacher's gifts, redundant as term was over and I'd missed last post. Stan immediately filled the bathtub. He'd missed his long soaks. Recently I'd begun to let him test the temperature and bathe unsupervised.

Hearing too few splashes, I checked and found him eyes closed, perilously close to nodding off in the steaming water. More vigilance required. Every bath time needed monitoring.

"More hot water top ups? You're getting out any minute now!"

"Actually Mum, I call this a top down!"

A long and earnest explanation followed about lifting the plug to drain cooler water, whilst adding more hot water. He leaned his foam-covered arms over the bath, "I don't want to get better too quickly, because I like all this extra attention from you."

If he could always find a positive, why couldn't I? *Relax*, I told myself. *Enjoy Christmas*. But my festive spirit was dented.

After New Year, Stan no longer feared the needle but had developed a routine to intimidate whoever was performing the procedure. I stood back while he instructed junior doctors on the perfect blood test.

It involved no magic cream "for babies!" No calling him *darling* or *dear*, an insistence on placing his arm where he could see it, about 30cm from his face. Once they'd accepted this awkward position, he continued making them nervous by watching the needle and requesting "No small talk, please."

By mid-January, Stan's platelets were back up to 132, and that was the number I told people who asked. There was so much I didn't tell. How, even with his platelets travelling in the right direction, my unease remained.

Good news felt temporary. Everything could change in a heartbeat, a second, a phrase of music, or even a few beats. Was the lesson to seize the day? Or that parenting Stan would probably always involve an element of holding my breath?

Although Stan's energy was better, my bath-side vigil continued. Covertly, my eyes examined his back. I feared battalions of tiny bruises would resume their march across his body but found none in the expanse of white skin. He splashed and sloshed, another top up or top down.

For Stan, ITP was simply another chapter of his legend, one where he got his fangs and overcame his fear of blood tests. I craved his resilience. The unexpected stone thrown into our water had sunk to the cloudy depths, but its ripples continued to permeate outwards.

Remember the Mayflies
Joshua Jones

It's cooler here, away from the throng of guests who smile and clink champagne flutes and sway to the band, a seven-piece jazz combo, crooning out another Louis Armstrong number. Nothing like the receptions back home, union hall affairs with someone's nephew DJing. The ground falls away here, at the edge, tumbles into gentle folds and then the inky ribbon of the Hudson. Above, a flotilla of Chinese lanterns, bobbing in the humid night. The river echoes the gauzy light, scatters it like luminous schools of fish. There are dozens of the lanterns, hundreds maybe, one for each guest. I carry mine, still unlit. A keepsake, I tell myself.

I see her through a gap of bodies. She's laughing with one of the maids of honor. I don't see Brian anywhere. More lanterns are lit, and everything smells of paraffin and sulfur. She smiles at my approach, then looks up to the constellation of drifting lights, her face almost childlike. The same expression she'd hold on Mayfly Nights, when we would lie together on the damp banks of the Mississippi, beneath a startling swarm of wings flickering in and out of the moonlight. I'd listen to her breathing, quiet below the raspy buzz of mayflies, how her breath would pause after each inhalation before releasing a slow whisper of air. I'd feel the heat of her hands, though we'd never touch, our fingers always a few centimeters from one another. And above us, delicate wings everywhere. Trillions, some say, as if such a number is possible. By sunrise, their beating would cease, and they would cover roads and cars and still-glowing neon signs, would be considered a blight.

"Remember the mayflies?" she asks, still looking at the lanterns.

"You'll have to take Brian someday," I say.

She casts about, spots Brian dancing with the groomsmen and passing a flask back and forth, says, "He doesn't like insects."

"Most people don't."

She takes the lantern from me although I didn't offer it and produces a lighter. Hers? Has she started smoking now, too? The wick catches; the lantern comes to life. When together we let the lantern go, it falters, threatens to slip along invisible air currents to the river below. Then the candle inside flares, glows bright, and it lifts and lifts to join the other lanterns.

"Most people," I say, but stop. I don't know how to finish, to say that most people would have said something long ago, but her eyes aren't on me anymore. Her head is tilted back, the night alive with light. Far above, the highest lanterns shimmer like mayflies. Then, one by one, the lights go out.

Unrolling the Dead Sea Scrolls

William Doreski

Something about the wind tonight
reminds me of archaeologists
unrolling the Dead Sea scrolls.

You must be infinity gentle
handling such brittle old texts.
Strange gods wrote or inspired them

to complicate religious views
established in arid climates
that preserve the ruins of many

overlapping ancient cultures.
But the wind isn't the voice
of any of those arrogant spirits.

It doesn't promise an afterlife
shaped like an oasis where
camels can replenish their humps

and travelers can exchange stories
about their favorite deities.
The wind doesn't care if you

believe its unfolding rhetoric,
doesn't worry that trees might fall
as it stomps across a landscape

of rough-cast, moon-gray shadows.
You've always wanted to visit
the biblical parishes sprawled

from Egypt east to Afghanistan,
but decades of war have rumpled
the maps, rechanneled the rivers,

scoured the ruins in the name
of the latest, greatest belief.
The wind can easily sift

rumor from reason. The scrolls
rest in museums, their contents
transcribed for scholars to parse

the way the wind parses forest
and keeps you tossing awake
with a thousand shabby threats.

CREATIVE NONFICTION SECOND PRIZE

What Nightmare is This?

Rachel Amegatcher

❧

BLACK LIVES MATTER
We see: Black lives
They see: Black matter
We get: Black bodies

When we scream "Black lives matter," we get thrown, slapped in our faces that "ALL LIVES MATTER! ALL LIVES MATTER!" Trust me, you don't have to yell. My heart has known that long before you felt the need to turn testimonies into mistakes you must correct. You know if you really believed all lives matter, you would add your voice to the choir and make us louder, not drown us out.

What nightmare is this?

When we fist Black lives matter, we're not saying all lives don't, we're reminding people that they do. When you say all lives matter, you pretend it's for equality while continuing to ignore a whole group of people who have not been equal for a long time. When something is for the Black community you try to make it for everyone, though when something is for you, it is yours exclusively. Why do you try to fight us when we speak out? Use the cracks of our bones to create beats for your drum?

What nightmare is this?

When we see you put on your armor and wield your swords, we make room beside us, but you draw a battle line and stand on the other side. And when someone yells to point out the enemy, you raise your arm and point to our faces. What nightmare is this, that people kiss their guns and curse their brothers? When will I wake up from a reality that values Black product more than Black people and will snatch Black money as fast as Black lives? "What can I say? Black money is still green!"

Growing up I imagined thunderstorms as gifts from God. The hammering rain, the belting thunder, the crescendoing lightning, all heaven's orchestra. The music, a sign, that He was in good spirts. Though someone once told me thunderstorms were God's tears. His great sorrows and deep pains. More and more I'm starting to believe that version of the story, because looking down on us now, God would have more to cry than smile about.

What nightmare is this?

Every time a new video of a murder springs up, it feels like a seed planted long ago that you only know about now because the fruit has flowered. But these videos are not flowers, they don't attract blue butterflies and golden honeybees. People don't take their sweet scent to make pink perfumes. They are not given to people to express "I love you." You're not surprised when you see another video. You're furious. You watch them after you make sure your heart is strong enough from the last heartbreak, and after you make sure you have bandages ready for the next one. You watch and say, "I can't believe they did that again. I can't believe they took that man's life."

What nightmare is this?

And you watch the White men who stole the Black man's breath. Watch the ease. The chill. The cool. It was so easy for them to shoot ripping bullets. It was so easy for them to suffocate final words. It was so easy for them to drag unconscious bodies. It was so easy for them to walk away.

Why?

Because their hearts overflow with hate, they do not know love. Because they know they can get away with it. Because they know they have people out there who support them, understand them, will stay quiet for them. But that's not us.

Whose nightmare is this?

Being Black in America. To those who don't know, to those who don't want to listen, I will be speaking with words they'll never understand, painting with colors they can't see, as if the colors came from a second rainbow that doesn't exist. Being Black in America, to wonder why some people despise you so much. I can't believe we are still trying to convince people we're human. You really hate me this much because of the color of my skin? Can't you see my eyes?

Whose nightmare is this?

Why do I have to scream Black lives matter? My throat hurts. Why can't you hear Black lives matter when we laugh? Why can't you feel Black lives matter in our touch? You watch us walk with, run toward, dance to, and you're telling me you still can't see Black lives matter? Don't you know we watch these videos and cry? That we fear for our parents and pray for our kids. That we're traumatized. That we're tired. And oh, the guilt. I'm the angriest, but the lives you took deserve angrier. Guilt. I'm crying, but the lives you took deserve a flood. Guilt. And oh, the irony. Guilt weighing heavier on these dry hands then on the ones you use to stain white walls red.

This is our nightmare.

The truth is I can't imagine hating a group of people as much as you hate us. I really cannot imagine having that on my heart . . . I just cannot imagine. The weight of it would crush my soul. Thank God I believe in better than you, otherwise there would be no hope. Your hate took Breonna Taylor. Your hate took Ahmaud Arbery. Your hate took George Floyd. May God give them rest at last. Your hate has stolen so many people. One day it will kill us all.

Wake up.

Mitochondrial Eve

Lisa M. Kendrick

When I was young I learned to bleed tears,
washing out my womb with every full moon.
I weathered hormones that stormed
with the blood, then flooded when it left,
fighting harder to carry lean muscle,
to run faster, to toss higher, to birth babies.

I ruled the greatest empires on earth,
channeled snakes to protect my kingdoms,
cut the hair of magicked warriors for family,
was turned to salt for independent thinking,
sold to crowds so the men could escape,
walked away from paradise for knowledge.

I strode from West Africa with a babe on my back
to Mother the last line of homo sapiens,
was raped by new gods, my daughters stripped
of even priestesses to comfort them.
I patched together brothers, served fathers,
fled from husbands, seduced lovers.

I once raised kingdoms with matrilineal lineage,
then watched them swallowed by bloated gods
who believe a fist is better than grain. Yet no deed
done in myth without my whispers from painted caves,
my image weaving beneath bent boughs, even kings
came to my lakes for enchanted swords: I was always there.

Slavery can't endure where women mold bridges
with baskets and the moon bends to knead waves.
Don't you hear the slither of silence: deals made
between women behind the backs of their masters?
The sonorous pitch that tickles eardrums
is the tide of patriarchy toppled with whispers.

I persist, like blood that falls with lunar shifts,
water cycles that wash the world clean,
wombs that raise babies with moon faces.
I have tucked your lash in amongst the linens,
and taught my daughters to shrink it in the wash,
knowing slavery withers where women braid baskets.

Mansplaining

Chris Gilmore

Man: So according to you, my charming wife, the standard definition is "when a man explains something to a woman that she already knows, in a condescending or patronizing tone." Which raises some questions. For one thing, it's impossible to know what anyone knows about anything, and it's arrogant to assume otherwise. So when I explained to you, the other day, who Beethoven was, I was simply trying to do you a favor. I was trying to be courteous. Did I *assume* that you knew anything about the greatest musical mind in the history of humanity? No. Because that would be presumptuous. So I gave you, out of the goodness of my heart, a brief tutorial—or, as you called it, a "tedious lecture"—about the earth-shattering impact of his genius—a lecture, by the way, that many people would find enlightening and be grateful to hear. But because it came from me, your loving husband, you found it "insufferable," not to mention "grounds for divorce." But if you had simply said, "Yes, I know who Beethoven is, and I'm aware of his artistic legacy," instead of saying—as I later found out, sarcastically—"No, I don't. Please tell me," we could have avoided the whole fiasco, and your grandmother's lamp would still be intact. Also, and perhaps more importantly, it's impossible to define a "condescending or patronizing tone." My tone, for instance, might occasionally *sound* condescending, but that doesn't mean it is. Chances are, you're just looking for an excuse to be offended. Has that ever occurred to you? Rhetorical question: I know it has. It's a mistake we all make, from time to time, but the important thing is to weigh the consequences of someone's actions against their intentions, which are usually innocent. I can't speak for others, but I can say with absolute certainty that nothing I do or say is *designed* to offend. However, if my actions somehow, for some reason, upset people, that's truly unfortunate—but hardly my fault. They should, as rational adults, be able to control their emotions. Wouldn't you say? Please correct me if I'm wrong. I don't think I am, but feel free to disagree. You know how much I value your opinion. And I apologize if I'm being pedantic. I know I have a tendency to rant when I get in the zone intellectually. I just want to be as clear and as thorough as possible. You probably don't know this—or maybe you do, I might've told you—but I *aced* my philosophy exam in high school. Just in case you were wondering how I became so adept at in-depth analysis. I could talk about mansplaining and its fallacies for days—as I'm sure you could, too. That's the point. We both have opinions on the subject, and I'm sure they overlap more often than not. But the only way we learn about them is by letting the other person speak, hearing their ideas, sympathizing with their perspectives. Listening—*really* listening—is key to understanding, don't you think? Dialogue, not monologue. Sharing, receiving, exchanging. Communion, in other words, with other minds. Hold on, I'm almost done. You can respond in a second. Ah dammit, I lost my train of thought. I was going to say something profound. Just a sec, it'll come back to me. While we wait, do you remember a few weeks ago when I explained the difference between a coffee and an Americano, and you hit me in the eye with a creamer? Well, at the time, I had no idea that you'd worked at Starbucks during grad school. How could I? You never told me. And the other day when I informed you that Henry James and William James were cousins, and you said—correctly, it turns out—that they were brothers, and you should know because you have a PhD in American Literature, I wasn't being condescending or patronizing. Sure, I may have adopted an "infantilizing tone," but I do that all the time—and, after eight years of marriage, I think you know that. When I sigh and roll my eyes and curse the heavens for sending me such a stubborn, misguided companion, I'm merely making a joke about my father, who used to say the same thing to my mother on a daily basis. If anyone was in need of a lecture on mansplaining, it was him, not me. I've learned from his mistakes, just as you've tried to learn from your mother's. I only say "tried" because you have your moments—very *occasional* moments—when I can see her ghost hovering in the subtext of our conversations, when you become obnoxious and verbose and long-winded. But those moments are rare indeed—which is why we're still married. God knows how little patience I have for such displays of self-satisfied indulgence. And I say that with love and respect for your mother, of course. You know how much I liked her. Even though she never liked me. At least, I don't think she did. It was hard to tell sometimes. People are incomprehensible, aren't they? Even now, it looks to me like you're boiling with rage—your face is red, your veins are popping, your eyes are narrow—but that's probably nothing more than a misinterpretation on my part, a misreading of social cues. There's no way to really know. I suppose I could just ask, but where's the fun in that? Human interaction is about irony and drama. Questions only spoil the mystique. Don't you agree? What am I saying? Of course you do. You're an English major. You know all about people saying the wrong thing at the wrong time in the wrong way, and all the available damage that such miscalculations can create. So, in short, I think we should avoid assumptions about what people may or may not know, whether they're interested in what you're telling them, whether your tone is condescending, or whether you're droning on and on like some clueless narcissist who doesn't know when—or how—to shut up. As you know, I try to be respectful whenever I speak. Respectful of time, respectful of feelings. But I'm well-aware that for every man like me, there are a dozen boorish buffoons in love with the sound of their voice. I don't have to tell *you* that, though. You've dated enough pompous windbags to know the difference. Needless to say—but I'll say it anyway, just to be perfectly clear—mansplaining exists. It happens every day, everywhere, and it's a travesty whenever it does. In fact, on behalf of my gender, I'd like to apologize for the men who are too blind, too self-obsessed and insensitive to recognize the crimes they're committing. I only hope that one day they'll be able and willing to change.

Woman: I just asked where you wanted to go for dinner.

Overheard after
Dr. Christine Blasey Ford

Janna Grace

Three men in their early twenties lean in
towards each other, close around a circular bar table
until I walk by, to the restroom.
It is tight, so I don't open the door all the way
and squeeze my body by.
They glance, unconsciously, a body part
each, or maybe two, and keep talking.

I hear one say how Kavanaugh was clearly bold—
a bold- faced liar that is,
and I grinned as I shut the door behind
and met myself in the mirror.
A pattern of a woman in a Victorian dress
being spanked,
legs splayed and dress upturned, repeated
up and down around my face and before
I could sit, one of the men laughed
and asked what "boofing" is.
My face fell and I wondered why I ever let it rise.
"When a bitch gets fucked up the ass," came the laughing reply.

I cried above the toilet and thought of her scientific explanation
of trauma
and how after, so many peoples' voices lifted
in pretend curiosity
in affectation, in veneer
when they asked, innocently, how she could forget
how she got home.

I had to squat and shake and then, after washing, dried
my hands on my skirt
because it was a woman's bathroom
so the only paper was on those walls.

I don't know how I got home the night I ran from my friend's party
barefoot.
I remember his teeth pushing mine and the back of my head
slamming into a headboard and Christine
I too will never forget
the laughter, I remember

the bits of gravel in my knees and the fat parts of my palms
and the one chunk stuck between my left pinky toe and whatever
the other toe is called,
when I stumbled down the stairs into the street.

But then,
I was in bed.

When I did walk out, I made sure they realized how close
I had been, swinging wide,
bumping the door into the back of one of their chairs.
He slid his in a touch, polite, and all three looked at me once
more.
This time my eyes held them
on my face, the part they skimmed
on their earlier journey,
sheet rock smeared with mascara.

I still wish I had known what to say.
I still don't.
But, my damp eyes did their best—
glint above a jaw like a beer
bottle hard and sharp and easy
to break.

"Do you like beer!?"

I did not wipe the tears because I will not hide how they make us feel anymore.

I will not give them another comfort or benefit
of the doubt. I will be Mrs. Ramsay at dinner and I will drown them all
at the lighthouse.

Walking home, a man said, seriously
to another man on the sidewalk:
"I need a stupid woman with no morals tonight."
I was alone and my body lives
so I kept moving. But, I sent a silent net out
to drag him down, my will an anchor
with a chain too short,
whispered to all my drunk sisters
of his soul.

There are no benefits of doubt here.
The two men didn't laugh
when they walked by
and they did not feel shame
because they had not seen me.
I had my coat on by then,
I wasn't really there.

Just Looking: A reflection on John Updike and what it means to write about art

Cynthia Close

John Updike taught me how to read. Not literally, he was just the first writer I discovered while still in high school that I wasn't forced to read for a class. *The Poorhouse Fair* was the book, the trigger, one of his earliest. I picked it up at a yard sale. He spoke to me in a voice I could hear. I was not an avid reader, but I fixated on Updike. *The Same Door*, a book of short stories, came next. I love the short story form because I have a short attention span that can't be blamed on early cellphone addiction, having been born in 1945. After that it was the fifteen-year-old narrator, Peter Caldwell, in *The Centaur*, a wanna-be artist, a painter who reflected the budding desires beginning to form in my own teenage heart.

My Gram supported my reading habit by giving me a new Updike book every Christmas, surprising since her own reading was confined to forays into pulp fiction, murder mysteries churned out with regularity by authors usually writing under a pseudonym. *Rabbit, Run* was her first choice. What a great book. There is something of me in Harry "Rabbit" Angstrom. I think it has to do with writing in your own time, writing in a voice that is very present in your own time. Joyce Carol Oates also filled my bookshelves in college but now I can't understand why. I also feel a tad smug knowing I was reading Margaret Atwood long before my erudite Mah Jongg playing buddies more recently signed up for Hulu to watch *Handmaid's Tale*. But even in this #MeToo moment, when some ardent feminists have tried to rub the shine from his reputation, accusing him of being a misogynist, no one ever quite replaced Updike in my ranking of writers.

I have read nearly everything Updike has written, and each book seemed to tell me something about where I was in my own life at that time. It was as though he'd been stalking me. The novel "*S*", his nod of acknowledgement to Nathanial Hawthorne considered one of his lesser works, was almost too close for comfort. Like the middle-aged female protagonist, I left everything to run off to a commune. The shallowness of her character, her vanity made me feel my own superficiality, my contentment with slipping over the surface of things so as not to slow myself down, not to get too encumbered with the "meaning" of life. I was too busy living.

More than a few years ago, my best friend at the time gave me *Just Looking*, Updike's first collection of essays on art. I was still a practicing artist back in 1989 when *Just Looking* was first published by Knopf. Although many of these essays had been published earlier in *The New Republic*, *The New York Times*, and *Vanity Fair* they were new to me. It was during a time in my life when I'd started to question the value of art making in general and more specifically the value of my own artistic production and its long-term impact on others.

Like me, Updike's first artistic interest was in drawing. At Harvard he was president of *The Harvard Lampoon*, contributing many cartoons, and writing much of the content. Besides Harvard, he also attended the Ruskin School of Drawing and Fine Art in Oxford, England. Updike dedicated *Just Looking* to his art teachers Clinton Shilling, Carlton Boyer, Percy Horton and Hyman Bloom. Bloom was the theoretical forefather of my art school education at Boston University dominated back in the 1960s and 70s by The Boston School, a group of figurative expressionists who provided an alternative to the cool emotional distance of minimalism and a bulwark to the abstract expressionist tidal wave of Pollack and de Kooning that had been gathering momentum since 1945.

My own work fell squarely in the Boston camp. It was my ability to draw the human figure that won my entrance to Boston University on a scholarship before I had any knowledge of Hyman Bloom, or minimalism. I was unaware of the Bloom connection between myself and Updike until I started rereading *Just Looking* as a way to help clarify my own transition from making art to writing about it. This time around I approached the book more as an investigator, searching for clues to unravel the mystery of myself. I read the dedication, something I usually pass over and don't remember reading the first time around, or maybe I did back then but at the time it didn't seem significant. Now, Updike's tribute to Bloom reverberated in a way that seemed beyond germane, it was prescient.

I'd been assigned by my editors at *Art + Object* to write a review of *Hyman Bloom: Matters of Life and Death* (July 13, 2019 – February 23, 2020), the first comprehensive exhibition of the artist's work at the Boston Museum of Fine Arts since his death at the age of 96 in 2009. I approached Bloom's work with a renewed interest, a combination of excitement tinged with regret. Afraid that in confronting these paintings, works that I had only experienced in reproduction projected in slides during an art history survey course in my student days, I would be painfully reminded of my self-aborted career as an artist. My paintings and drawings had begun to attract some attention from curators in Boston in the 1980s. Old friends and early admirers of my artwork were surprised and confused when I blithely informed them, "I've given up painting." Saying it was an "easy" decision does not feel quite honest. More so at the time, it felt necessary.

I don't think Updike ever fully invested himself in believing he was destined to be an artist as I had. Cartooning and caricature à la *The New Yorker* served as his adult artistic playground. In *Just Looking*, he refers to himself as an "adolescent cartoon buff" and he devotes "A Case of Melancholia," the most detailed and extensive essay in the book, to a deep rendering of the cartoonist Ralph Waldo Barton (1891-1931) who was featured in *The New Yorker Album of Drawings 1925-1975*. I skipped this essay the first time around. In my personal hierarchy of artistic endeavor, cartooning was way below my eye level. I literally couldn't "see" it. This time I read the essay about Barton. Updike paints a colorful, penetrating portrait in words of this extravagant man who was the most popular caricaturist of his time, publishing his drawings in *Puck*, *Judge*, *Life*, *Harper's Bazaar*, *The Cosmopolitan* and *Vanity Fair*. At his peak he was being paid fifteen hundred dollars for a single drawing for publication and once he did eighty-five drawings in one week. A pretty astounding amount even by today's standards and this was in New York in the 1920s.

Although Updike opens the Barton essay with a full page, overtly racist illustration of a New York City trashman, he does not call the artist out in those terms. In 1989 racism was not on the tip of everyone's tongue, an epithet to be hurled about accusingly as it is today but instead Updike describes the drawing's effect as being, "oddly intense, with something malevolent in the rendering of the trashman's simian limbs, drooping gargoylish head, fangs, pop eyes, and crazily lolling tongue." In analyzing the aesthetic approach, apart from the content, Updike calls our attention to Barton's sophisticated composition: "But in Barton the background presses toward the foreground with an insistence found in Oriental art and again in Cubism." Early in the essay Updike dives headlong into Barton's life: "Barton was married four times and fathered two daughters–Natalie by the first wife, née Marie Jennings and by his second wife, Anne Minnerly (who next married E.E. Cummings), a second daughter, Diana. His third wife, the actress Carlotta Monterey, became Eugene O'Neill's third wife, and Barton's fourth wife, Germaine Taileferre, was a well-known French composer–a member, with Poulenc and Milhaud, of *Les Six*. One month after his fourth divorce was final, and a few days after Carlotta had returned from Europe with O'Neill, Barton committed suicide, three months short of his fortieth birthday."

Suddenly Updike has grabbed my attention. The drawings and cartoons that had barely tickled my interest have now become evidence in deciphering this man, and perhaps looking more intently to see how his life was reflected in his art. Updike's essay takes on a distinctly journalistic tone. His statement of facts reads like a police procedural: "Around midnight on May 19th, 1931, in his penthouse apartment at 419 East Fifty-seventh Street . . ." Updike describes in great detail the circumstances surrounding the artist's death—he shot himself with a gun he'd bought specifically for that job—and then Updike backtracks into a vivid, gossipy account of Barton's short, tumultuous life, unrolling the artist's often painful, ego-driven eccentricities made visible through his creative output. By the end of the essay Updike had taught me a lesson in how to see the clues in an artist's body of work that ultimately helps to understand their life whether or not you found the work appealing.

In the introduction to *Picked-Up Pieces*, a 1975 collection of essays, Updike listed his personal five rules of literary criticism, which can easily serve the same purpose in writing about art if you substitute "artist" for "author" and instead of "book" think "work of visual art":

1. "Try to understand what the author wished to do, and do not blame him for not achieving what he did not attempt.
2. Give enough direct quotation—at least one extended passage—of the book's prose so the review's reader can form his own impression, can get his own taste.
3. Confirm your description of the book with quotation from the book, if only phrase-long, rather than proceeding by fuzzy précis.
4. Go easy on plot summary, and do not give away the ending.
5. If the book is judged deficient, cite a successful example along the same lines, from the author's œuvre or elsewhere. Try to understand the failure. Sure it's his and not yours?

To these concrete five might be added a vaguer sixth, having to do with maintaining a chemical purity in the reaction between product and appraiser. Do not accept for review a book you are predisposed to dislike, or committed by friendship to like. Do not imagine yourself a caretaker of any tradition, an enforcer of any party standards, a warrior in any ideological battle, a corrections officer of any kind. Never, never . . . try to put the author "in his place," making of him a pawn in a contest with other reviewers. Review the book, not the reputation. Submit to whatever spell, weak or strong, is being cast. Better to praise and share than blame and ban. The communion between reviewer and his public is based upon the presumption of certain possible joys of reading, and all our discriminations should curve toward that end."

"Better to praise and share than blame and ban." How kind, how genial and how unlike many art and literary critics who had come before him. I have a tendency to make snap judgments, a character flaw conditioned by the speed that has propelled me through life. Patience is not one of my virtues along with more than my share of perhaps irrational self-confidence.

In 2008, the year before his death, Updike gave the National Endowment for the Humanities' prestigious Jefferson Lecture, titled "The Clarity of Things: What Is American About American Art?" In that lecture he retraces some of the same ground he covered in *Still Looking,* his 2005 second collection of essays on art, this time specifically American art. I recently added this book to my Updike shelf. In describing Jackson Pollock, a most American and—still for many—a suspect artist whose work defies classification, Updike captures the very heart of these mystifying images ". . . in dots and lines and little curdled clouds of dull color, of the cosmos . . . It is all line, dribbled and spattered in an ecstatic dance in the mystic space between concept and thing." And here is where Updike has led me, *Still Looking* and now using words, instead of splatters of paint to more patiently make my own way finding the connections between concepts and things, life and art.

* * *

Addendum: John Updike has won many literary prizes, awards, and honors, including the Pulitzer Prize, the National Book Award, and the National Book Critics Circle Award, twice each; the Pen Faulkner Award for Fiction, the Rea Award for the Short Story; and a Guggenheim Fellowship. He is among a select few to have received both the National Humanities Medal and the National Medal of Arts.

Appointment. Psychic Surgeon. Manila. 1972.

Alison Clare

Nadia had first heard about the Great Surgeon at the Peoples Temple. She thought little of Jim Jones' theatrics, and thankfully so had her mother, Yana. The frenzied congregation was a thrumming hive of eager believers, if not in Jones, or his God, then certainly in some kind of world of miracles. Yana was adept at seeking out others as equally desperate for divine intervention and as they left the church, one bony hand clutching at her stomach, as she now always did, she showed her daughter a crumpled piece of paper, a name and address scrawled across it in thin blue ink. Nadia had taken note of the Philippines address with little concern. Yana moved from the idea of one quick cure to another, from day to day. On that particular hazy San Francisco morning, Yana's faith had been in the square firmly upon the promises of the Peoples Temple. By lunch time, she was enamored with the legend of the Great Surgeon.

The smell of eucalyptus oil made Nadia's eyes burn. The Great Surgeon was liberal in its application to her mother's naked stomach, and the urge to cover her own eyes, nose, and throat was overwhelming. It was a hundred degrees in the shade, one hundred percent humidity outdoors, and anything but a light sundress against her skin was unthinkable, so Nadia didn't have anything to press over her face to block the stench. A nurse, hovering by Nadia's side, offered up a small hand towel. Grateful, she took the cloth, ignoring the filthy edges, grey with repeated use and poor washing. She blanched when the towel met her nose, her eyes watering at the repeated onslaught of more eucalyptus oil. Nadia let the towel hang between limp fingers and stared up at the cracking ceiling, blinking at the stinging moisture. She imagined flakes of old paint falling from above and onto the operating table.

The Great Surgeon's operating room was a far cry from the San Francisco hospital where her mother, Yana, had been diagnosed with cancer. The consulting room there had been pristine and white, antiseptic in its cleanliness. There was nothing hygienic at all about the Great Surgeon's so-called hospital. The makeshift surgery in Manila was dark and filthy, the large group of wide-eyed American patients crammed into the mustard-yellow waiting room sitting together on dusty old couches and drinking warm soda out of cracked mugs. Yana lay now on a bare metal table, draped in red cotton blankets. A deep, blue clay bowl had been positioned by her head, partially covered by a thin sheet of muslin, ready to catch the cancer when it was extracted.

The Great Surgeon leaned over his patient. "Ready, Mrs. Yana?"

The assisting nurse stood for a moment in front of Nadia, guiding her back from the operating table, obstructing her view. When the nurse joined the surgeon at his side, he was already poised to begin work, knife in hand.

The scalpel met her mother's skin and Nadia was almost relieved when her vision blurred at the sight. The blade disappeared behind the Great Surgeon's clenched fingers where he had placed them against Yana's stomach, obstructing the view of the first cut. Blood immediately welled around the heel of his hand where it pressed hard against the curve of Yana's swollen belly. Nadia averted her eyes, staring instead at her mother's face. Yana's eyes were closed and but for the odd twitch of a muscle below her right eye, she appeared to feel no pain. She inhaled suddenly, a longer, sucking breath, and Nadia's knees jolted, ready to rush to her mother's side.

The Great Surgeon yanked one hand into the air, holding it high with a cry of victory. Held tight in his fist, a bloody mass of muscle and sinew bled furiously, the red running down his wrist and forearm. Nadia stared at his blood-soaked hand, captivated. The nurse clapped her hands and bounced on her bare feet. The Great Surgeon grinned at Nadia, exposing three shining gold teeth. His smile was unkind, vicious. She suspected he knew that Nadia had doubted him: Yana might have even told him that her daughter thought him a quack. But now here he was, a hunk of bleeding tissue extracted from her mother's stomach clenched in his filthy hand. Nausea swept up the length of her throat and Nadia fought the urge to vomit. One hand over her mouth, she fled the room.

Nadia burst into the hallway and was instantly lost as her eyes burned. She stumbled, knocking against the wall, searching for the waiting room. It had been, she thought, just outside the operating room, but she had clearly exited the wrong door. Nadia pulled at the first door handle she saw and fell through the opening into a dark grey room. The walls were badly water damaged and the smell of mold was heavy in the air. A fluorescent tube buzzed above Nadia's head. Blinking into the bright light, she stared in horror at the sight of a man standing at a steel table, hands deep inside the entrails of a dead chicken. A bloody knife lay on the table beside the carcass.

The man had slit the chicken open from neck to tail and wrenched the bird in half. A handful of deep, blue clay bowls sat on the table beside the man's work, each filled with bloody organs. On the floor beside his sandaled feet, a pile of dead chickens had been heaped into a reed basket. The table and the cement floor around it were covered with blood and feathers. The man stared back at her in shock, his black eyes wide. Nadia knew that she was not supposed to be here.

She backed out of the room and tripped on her own feet as she tried to run away. With a startled cry, she tried to right herself and fell straight into a soft body. The nurse who had overseen her mother's procedure steadied Nadia with tiny hands. Noticing the open doorway behind Nadia, the nurse's smooth forehead pinched, but she closed the door without comment. Unconcerned by Nadia's clammy skin and panting breath, she smiled and pointed back down the hall, beckoning Nadia to follow.

The nurse led Nadia into a different room. Seated on a large armchair at its center, Yana sat upright with a light blanket draped across her waist. She was pale and blinked repeatedly with encroaching sleep, but smiled when Nadia entered. At Yana's side, the Great Surgeon stood, his white shirt stained with blood and sweat. His hands were now clean, and in the circle of one fist, he held a wad of American money.

"It worked," said Yana when Nadia knelt before her. "The cancer is gone." She peeled back the blanket to reveal the unblemished skin of her stomach. It was pale and smooth, lifting and falling gently with Yana's breath. Nadia had expected to see stitches. There were none.

Nadia rested her hands over Yana belly and imagined the vast network of tumors interlaced across her mother's stomach. She saw in her mind's eye the grey, dirty room down the hall: the blue bowls full of chicken entrails. She clutched at her mother's cold fingertips and tried to smile.

Wild Thing

Lisa Taylor

I pedaled around the *S,*
airborne over a tender mud hump,
before landing in the brook,
with bellows of toads,
and dragonflies flitting in cursive.

Everything afire, the jewel-edged scab
on my knee, pollen parachuting
over bluets, a dachshund sniffing rainbow oil
abutted by sand
I dented repeatedly
with my tires.

Each rotation brought
an uphill freedom
taking me farther than permitted,
beyond the muscular world of childhood,
out of earshot of growling voices
bisecting air,
the breezeway door groaning.

A straight-backed chair awaited me,
filtered light latticing my dinner plate,
and I bowed my head
mouthed the words to *Wild Thing*
mossy syllables transmuted into prayer.

In carbon black,
I ladder-climbed inside my bunk,
pulled bits of yarn and sticks
around me,
while moths gaudy as dahlias
dust-battered the screen.

Speeding

LA Patterson

The night air smells of danger and gunpowder. Inky pine tree silhouettes blur as the pickup truck kicks up white dust. The Chevy rattles its bones across the lime-rock road. My best friend and I slide around in the center of the slippery vinyl bench seat. A Winchester stretches on the gun rack behind our feathered and lacquered hair.

Two good old boys, country and western bookends, are on either side of us, the back pocket of their Wranglers tattooed by round tins of Copenhagen. The driver pilots the truck like a NASCAR racer, his pointy-toed boot heavy on the pedal.

We cut up as we work our way through a fifth of Lord Calvert, shouting above the skirl of motor and wind, making good time to nowhere.

"Buddy-ro," says the driver to his friend riding shotgun. "Reach into that glove box and hand me them black beauties."

His buddy produces a bagful of obsidian capsules and offers the speed like redneck communion.

Drunk and Digging

Mickey Mahan

Rocky The Flying Squirrel he ain't
staggering across the gas station lot
opposite side of the street
earflaps on his fur hat flapping
in mock take-off
and I'm wondering if he'll make it
to this side without getting run over
gesticulating for the bus with unhinged arms

I pull the bus to the curb and wait
don't ask me why
"thanks a lot my friend" he slurs
through an unkempt white beard almost bewitching
as it sparkles with snow
that face has chased down more than one bus
in its day
as he steadies himself on the sidewalk
staring up at me through floating eyes
I wonder which step will be his last

how close will he come to boarding the bus
before he breaks his neck
so when he's standing beside the driver's seat
staring down at me I think
"I'll be damned he did it"
and spitting out something resembling
"I'll be with you in a minute"
his feathery body drops into the front seat
as I pull away from the curb
with a reluctant foot and a wary eye

out of the corner of my eye
I watch him fiddle with his billfold
so thick you'd think he had more strings attached
than a flock of kites
and I'm wondering at what left hand turn
he's going to slide off the seat and crack his skull
in the bus aisle
"I'll be with you in just a minute buddy
just give me a minute I've got it here somewhere"
this can't be the first minute this old goat's
dug for something that isn't there
I'm wondering how often he's come up empty
but has still managed to oil his joints with alcohol
what kind of shaman's dance is he doing
on the edge of that bus seat
rocking back and forth in liquored resolve

we knock down the city blocks
with him teetering and me tensing
until we reach downtown
last stop
everybody off
and he's elbow deep
digging in his pockets
begging me
"please buddy just another minute
I know it's here somewhere"
and in a couple of tittering tipsy steps
he descends and lands on the sidewalk
feet as firmly planted as a telephone pole
and I think
"I'll be damned he did it"

Excerpts from the Classified Ads Section of Esoteric Creatures Monthly Magazine

Justin A.W. Blair

Middle-aged Vampire Seeks New Familiar

Specifics of the pact can be negotiated after initial acceptance by both parties. Normal terms apply, minimum commitment of a millenium, good references where possible. Prefer appearance of a furry nature — no wasps, insects or reptiles, please. Must be on-call for summoning anytime. Work mainly nights. Knowledge of lesser arcana required. Should know basics of Microsoft Office suite and experience with social media a plus. Ability to work in low light conditions. Contact ASAP.

Graveyard.

Mummy Requires History Lessons/Van with Tinted Windows

Listing is for two distinct tasks with preference given to applicant who can perform both.

First, I require an expert to discern my provenance and name. Exhibit label reads: Unknown Mummy, 100BCE-151BCE.

I don't think this is correct.

Applicant must be able to read hieroglyphs, Greek and Hieratic script. Degree from institution of higher learning preferred. Field experience in archaeology with corresponding immunity to ancient curses a huge asset.

Second, I require safe transport from museum grounds where I am currently located.

A little bit about the employer:

Recently, I awakened to find myself imprisoned in a museum display. I wander the darkened corridors at night, various bandages rapidly deteriorating, especially around armpit area and groin. Be aware, I walk very slowly in a halting step. Must be able to distract or neutralize security guard who works night shift. New guard is cagey, as I accidentally strangled the former one.

Museum of Fine Arts. Massachusetts.

Seeking Novice Ventriloquist with Suitably Submissive Attributes

Hi.

My name is Andy.

Looking for a Ventriloquist to go on the road. Work small county fairs in rural areas, rodeos and private parties. Have extensive rolodex of show business contacts from former partner. I dismissed him with extreme prejudice for constantly eating pork rinds while I sat on his lap as well as for wanton disobedience to my evil will. (If this sounds like you, please do not apply)!

I demand respect from my partner and brook no opposition to my infernal designs but I'm also really easy to get along with and a fun sidekick. Good conversationalist. Will talk for hours on many subjects while travelling. Eventually you will hear my voice inside your mind even when my mouth is not moving. Upside is you will never feel alone.

 Light weight. Easy to carry.

Let's get this show on the road!

555-555-3845

Wanted: Freelance Exorcist

I accidentally possessed a young gentleman who works in investment banking. It was a spur of the moment type thing. Usually, I go for girls on the cusp of puberty.

I was duped! The one occupied has no soul at all as I realized upon first seating myself upon the hollow throne of his immortal soul. There was nothing to claim, to mutilate or suborn.

He gets up on time every day. He goes to work. He smiles. His family appears outwardly normal. They smile. The kids play football. He gives money to various charities and is a member of the Chamber of Commerce.

I cannot escape him. His soul is an illusion. It's cold here . . . so cold. I cannot fathom the malevolence of anyone who would play such a dastardly game.

I've existed for one hundred thousand millennia and I have never been simultaneously so afraid and so bored. He sits in front of a screen watching numbers all day with the same smiling face.

I need you to exorcise me from this monster's body. I don't think he will even notice if you do it quickly. But to be fair, there may be some danger involved if I am correct that he planned this all along. Sometimes in the crazed corridors of this wretched human's mind I hear other demons, trapped here for years warning me, screaming out, laughing.

I know we don't usually work on the same side but I'm begging you defrocked priests, ministers without a flock, anyone, please! Get me out of here. I'll do anything. I'll listen to all the Bible verses you want. Just get me out.

Please, vanquish me back to hell.

New York, New York.

Evil Clown Needs Inspiration

Just like it says in the headline. I lost my verve. Looking for somebody or some *thing* to work with to get it back, see?

Usual stuff. Senseless murder and more murder, mainly. Appearing in forested areas during day to astonish passersby and children, then the serious stuff once it gets dark.

Honestly, I've just kind of lost my way. Don't know where the gumption went to get up and go KILL, KILL, KILL. Looking for a murderous clown with more spunk but less know-how to mentor. We can do each other's makeup.

I'll show you how to inspire terror in a small-town community. You show me what it feels like to be young again.

Contact: Klowns Killing It Talent Agency.

Ode to Dreaming in the Bathtub

Mark Gregory Lopez

I don't do it often,
but when it happens, the sky
relieves me of bones,
springs fins from knuckles
and stings my eyes, bits of
onion my mother water-shines
for the *pico de gallo*.
I tangle below the surface,
ignite melted flesh from skin-
trapped cells pelted and pink.
I'm not used to sinking,
but it happens when my feet
pierce the surface and walk
along the bathtub for three hours.
I do this before midnight.
I do this before the clock
limbers tendons
in the living room, my father's
cracked ribs click into soap-
scrubbed palms grasping television
prayer circles in 100-degree
seats, melted leather funneling
the drain back into my spine.
When I swallow
the Gulf of Mexico in sleep,
I count oil-soaked corpses
the local refineries
dribbled into the mouth of
the Atlantic, her body spitting me out
as I take her in, my back slipping along.
I used to eat fiberglass
in the shower before glistening
strands of rain-water

asked me to sit within her shoulder,
pluck flies from her black hair.
I birthed babies in the water,
painted them brown and bloody
like severed flowers in a crystal vase,
faces short-changed and hollowed out.
I counted them as water moccasins
swirled my feet in the Nueces River during Easter.
I gave them my eggs, plucked a bolt
from Jesus' hand and buried it in the dirt.
Now he sleeps with one hand at his side.
When I blow bubbles toward the faucet,
he catches them in his mouth,
saying we do this to remember
what it feels like to breathe.

The Wombat Hole

Nora Kirkham

The first time I heard my family was moving to Australia, I sprung into a spinning cartwheel along the front lawn of our rented house in Pennsylvania, where my father was on a temporary assignment. We moved to a house by the sea where we could see the Sydney Harbor from nearly any room. My two sisters and I arrived at our new private girls' school in uniform: mandatory yellow ribbons tied around hair-sprayed ponytails, Clark's, plaid wool skirts. My uniform hung on the door of my wardrobe every night, providing an identity that began to feel natural to slip into. Our new classmates asked us to pronounce *tomato* and *aluminum* and *aqua*. I said the words the way I always have, until I grew tired of their laughter and began to echo their sounds like a magpie. Now on the weekends, I walk to the beach and toss oily chips to seagulls. I coast underwater along the blue tiles of our pool until my fingers are white and wrinkled.

I only return to America once. We begin celebrating thanksgiving in July, simply because our kitchen is too hot in November for a turkey. I open the door during a heatwave in January and am smothered by a wild desert heat. We move our framed photographs away from windowsills. The sun bleaches their ink until our friends and family back in America look like ghosts. After dinner, my parents speak about other countries we could move to, places like Budapest or New Delhi or Brussels. I decide change is the worst thing that could happen to someone.

The objects in my room begin to take on talismanic, permanent stations. A jade rabbit sits on the same corner of my vanity until its back is caked in dust and a Japanese shell stays closed. If someone enters my room and moves these objects, my heart quickens. And now, my mother allows me to look at the book she bought for my older sister, a book about girls and their changing bodies. I sneak glances at the shy, watercolor illustrations of blood and new hair and hips as if landing upon a filthy secret. This will never happen to me.

At twelve, I am rapt with a sense that there are many things to be afraid of, and I am equally aware that I may not have the choice to hide from these things. I am terrified of the huntsman spider that bends its furry legs across the upper corners of my bedroom. I hold in my breath as it clings silently to the white wall. The silence between us prickles my chest as I imagine each of its eight legs folding until it falls onto my neck and bites me. I call for my father in a near whisper and he enters my room with a vacuum to steer the huntsman into a black hole.

When the sand begins to simmer under my feet, I leave Sydney, southbound on a school camping trip. For a week, we pitch tents under gum trees. In the mornings, the rain shakes minty oil from eucalyptus leaves. Its mist washes over the fabric of our hot little shelters.

We spend afternoons trekking over rocks and thick roots, clambering onto the sandstone shelves of caverns, blending clay and water between our fingertips. We draw red and brown lines across our sunburned arms and along our cheekbones, over the bridges of our noses. We sing, *kookaburra sits in the old gum tree* and the kookaburra seems to cackle at us between the giant ferns. We are perpetual trespassers, half-imagining ourselves native to a land that was never ours to begin with.

As if my pale complexion concealed under the weight of Australian mud isn't enough, I am an American, and the daughter of a diplomat. We ventured out of Maine when I was barely two years old. Moving ever since, we dodged winters and mastered the skill of inhabiting strange spaces, repeatedly asking them to welcome us. I've learned to shuffle through tone, language and mannerisms, alternating my expressions according to company. This is my third year in Australia, and the sharper tones of my American accent have flattened out. I sing in long, summery vowels.

When the British discovered Australia, they called it *Terra Nullius. Nobody's Land.* In school, we are taught that this, of course, was a myth. There was never a fuller land, splattered in heat and Dream Time fingerprints; white spots scattered like Southern Hemisphere stars across wood and stone. The sun is irresistible; the land is sweet and dangerous. Our teachers reprimand us when we leave the classroom without a hat. They keep large dispensers of sunscreen at their desks all year long. At the beach, we don't swim past the shark nets. In the bush we stomp on trails to alert the snakes, the red bellied and the sleeping king browns, warm and coiled. We float over sandy water, not knowing we are so small on this vast island, so strange to the current. When we are shown how to forage the Australian bush, I snap the ends of fuzzy ferns off their stems and chew them in the back of my mouth until my stomach twists and my eyes burn and I stagger back to the tent, clutching my abdomen.

I am alarmed by heights, and the zip-line my classmates and I fly across at the camp. But in front of this group of schoolgirls, the concept of option is nearly non-existent in our vocabulary. There is a zip-line stretched high across trees over a field. We must climb the ladder and fly across it. If you choose not to, you will be alone. We must have friends, we must grow taller, we must begin to embrace the swelling shapes of our bodies and jump.

So, I must go through the wombat hole. It is a hollowed-out underground maze of earth, consisting of layers of fluffy soil camped on packed clay. Before we even boarded the bus, we spoke of the Wombat Hole as a rite of passage, each of us uttering its name with a shudder as we tugged on our cotton dresses. Our teachers want us to challenge ourselves, but it will be a dirty task. Dressed in our fathers' old t-shirts, each girl prepares to enter the hole by crawling on her stomach. It is pitch black inside, with one corner cut open to the sunlight. Our eyes will adjust to the darkness and we will use our elbows to edge along the corners of earth. Odd metal objects from an old farm have been lodged into the ground. We must slip around these too.

Girl after girl squirms and peers into the black tunnel before sliding under the overpass like a newborn animal. I stand on the edge of the group, listening for any shout or sound that may have pushed its way up through the grass growing above the mound, waiting for a face to emerge on the other side. Soon enough, a chin appears above the soil. They must dig their way out. I watch fistfuls of dirt spray from their white knuckles as they reemerge. I wonder if this is really optional, if this cruel exercise is even worth boasting about. When my requests to decline this opportunity are laughed off, I beg the teacher for a head torch, and then for a friend to come alongside me. I pace until she concedes, and so I await the approaching minute when I have no choice but to look forward and shrink myself into the spaces of everything I cannot understand.   *

The day I go into the Wombat Hole, I am still small. I am one of the smallest girls in my class. If the tall girls can bend down and reach their way through, so can I. But I only enter because I have a light. I talk to my friend through the whole, uncertain route. Our elbows stir through soft waves of soil until we arrive at a corner where we stop, folded. Above is a wire patch sifting the sky. Light has never caused such a stillness in me. I feel as if we've been traveling underground for years. Outside there is the freedom of trees.

"There will be a time when I leave," I tell my friend. We hold hands loosely through the Wombat Hole. I can feel her legs kicking through the darkness behind me. At night, we'll howl like wolves from our tent, our lips spread open to flies. She won't be leaving. She will stay on through senior school and do her exams and attend university here. There will be more speech day ceremonies and beach days and New Year's Eves on the harbor.

How could it feel like the death my mother says leaving a place is? On my last day of school, I retreat to the restroom and feel the floor heaving. Something is shifting, spinning. My shoes are untied. I take long breaths to slow down my heart.

I don't know when the exit out of the hole becomes visible. The clay and soil are piled especially high, and we peel back torn roots and cobwebs with our arms. We are so eager to crawl back into the sun. I dig myself out with flecks of dirt between my teeth and red elbows. When I look back at that mound of earth, I wonder how I ever moved beneath it. This is the space I will never return to.

I planted a sapling once in a field that seemed to roll on forever. I wonder how tall it is now. I've said I would return to that field, but I probably never will. If I ran down that hill, I would be lost in a thousand trees planted since I left. Would it even matter which one I had planted, or would I be content to inhale their oxygen all at once? I would be standing over a gathering of infinite roots, as dizzying as stars swinging through the Milky Way.

We leave Australia two years later. My last meal is a mango, hastily cut by my neighbor who has stopped by to see us off. I hear the van rolling too quickly towards our house on the dead end as mango juice bleeds down my arm. When we pull away, I don't cry. The ceramic chipped number of our house vanishes behind me. I let the white lighthouse and the cliffs disappear. The rainbow lorikeets seem to speed away. Their green silky tails vanish behind me, too. I have dried juice all over my hands and knees.

We move to Boston, splintered, in the middle of winter. One of my sisters will leave for boarding school in Maine. I share a bed with my younger sister in a two-bedroom apartment as my parents prepare for our next assignment in Bucharest, Romania.

For six months, we don't go to school. Instead, we spend our afternoons walking along snow piled sidewalks towards the public library where I gather books about Europe in my arms. My sister and I fight, shouting things like "We hate America!"

I wake up in the night and sketch the blueprint of our house in Sydney, tracing its cool entrance, winding stairs, even the snails that glued themselves to our patio after rain. I imagine running to the house and collapsing on my knees, hammering on the door to be let back in. Other nights, I slink into my parents' room, heavy with anxiety.

Then I move to Romania and four years later, I fold up my life and move back to Boston for college. I later move to Switzerland, Russia, Ireland, Japan. There is a lorikeet feather in a box somewhere. There is a scar above my nose from a beach sunburn. One night, as the snow falls in Boston, as it always does, someone will ask me about Australia for the first time and I will unravel.

I wonder if one day the Wombat Hole will be packed in with fresh layers of mud. Maybe no one else will crawl through it, live for a moment so close to the beating earth. I listen to the years and simply let my body change. I pack up my life and unpack it. But I remember digging towards that light. It was inching closer; I could see a speck of it burning through the grains.

When I am twenty-two and living in Boston, my older sister is engaged to an Australian and moves back to Sydney. Though her plans are set, it seems to happen quickly. None of us had expected to ever return. We know that to return to an old home is a privilege.

By now, I have spent the past nine years sharpening my accent, unconsciously shedding any hint I lived in Sydney until the country alone is a concept, a great mass of floating land where I once walked. I listen to Americans speak of Australia, mainly commenting on its dangerous creatures. *Terra Nullius.* Again, I am made to explain the unlikelihood that they would suddenly be mauled by a shark the day they arrive.

I remember my version of Australia. Yes, it is covered in shiny blue jellyfish that can wrap themselves around your fingers until you feel like lightning has shot through your hand. It is bustling with cackling kookaburras and those shimmering, snaking rivers that soaked into my skin, but were unable to seep out. Nine years. I repeat this passage of time to myself and to those around me, as if asking them to understand why I could be so apprehensive about a return. It has been nine whole years since leaving. I am gripped with fear that I will go there and won't want to return to Boston, or a fear I will hate it. What does that light feel like again?

When I land in Sydney for the first time in nine years, it is the light I look for on the trunks of palm trees. Now I see how colorful the world I left behind is, slippery, green, and fragrant. I step over flattened frangipani flowers and tuck a fresh one behind my ear. The next time we drive to our old house on the dead end, I know this reality. It is brighter than I remember. This is still my home, along the sea and under the ground. I will relearn the waves with a secret in my hands: I have crawled close to the core of a farewell on the spinning earth. I can find my way back through its dim and surprising passages.

Where the Soil Is Soft

Cooper Young

My father wants to make a graveyard for poets,
and the field by our house would be the perfect place.
Rows of fruit trees used to line the old orchard,
but all that's left is an apple tree, a pear tree,
and two hollow plum trees that still bear fruit.

For each poet, he would bury a pinch of their ashes,
and pick a poem to engrave on their tombstone.
My father knows enough poets, but it's too late
to ask most of them, and no one wants to be
the first person buried in a graveyard.

Dad bought the property when he was still young,
and my brother, Jake, grew up in the little shack there.
The rough wooden floors gave him splinters when he learned to crawl.
To Jake, it was normal to put out pots and pans to catch rain,
which found its way through the cracks in the roof.

When my mother was pregnant with me,
a redwood fell through our home in a storm.
The sound of hammers and drills were my lullaby
as my father rebuilt the house with the wood from the fallen tree.
The redwood fell from "up on top,"

Our nickname for the field on the hill above our house.
When we were old enough,
that's where our father taught Jake and me to drive.
In that field, we learned how to prune an apple tree,
hunt for chanterelles, and turn over a garden.

Lately my parents have been threatening
to sell the house and move to a place
that's easier to grow old in. They're afraid
of making extra work for my brother and me.
They've always been like that.

Even when he's dead,
my father doesn't want to be a hassle.
He tells us to melt what's left of him to ash
and bury it "up on top,"
where he knows the soil is soft.

Meaning

Tuhin Bhowal

"The true meaning, ready to be decoded.
What never added up will add up,
What was incomprehensible will be comprehended."
— Czesław Miłosz

for Joie

Eating each other is the only way we learn to love.
The last man's name you garbled love for means *peace* in Urdu
—asylum, refuge; your viscous cannabis breaths still fresh as a
cut on my shoulders. In Bombay, he slurped into you like a
hungry child luridly sucking out from a shell, his cannibal
disquiet agog to mince the coconut. There must have been
another man afterwards but how does it matter. I gauged distance
between you and *peace*, which is to say between you and *years*—in
an undignified tongue. Even a decade ago, when I used to sneer at
Baba accusing him of naming me after his best friend from
college, how he had named his son the same—two years older to me
(and fairer) his face would turn bland like a poorly memorized
Bhutanese chicken recipe. He stood out for Tagore at the edge
of a poet's lushest gorge against the winds; I at the contour
of your bed against time. He picked up the noun from *Shesher Kobita*
– its setting the backdrop of Shillong. *Though, he wrote it in Bangalore.*
This city snorts in me now. *Abandoning home is imperative, after all,*
he often mumbled. That was his decade of denial. My name means
white—ultramarine to sound robustly pretentious. My skin a
turmeric ebony. My name means thin—the layers almost always
invisible over water buoyed by the pressure of my papery weight.
My name means brittle—I break easily, as easily as cherry blossoms
sprinkle over Sohra, as easily as oil levitates over a denser fluid,
as easily as icicles of Laitlum glitter against the moonshine in
Jogeshwari, as easily as a man can fail in love with one of the women
inside you. At poetry readings, when people ask what my name

means, I seldom explain. I neither mention Baba nor Tagore.
I don't recall if the last man's name you were in love with meant
peace when all you did was haunt each other like two apparitions
out of a chthonic machine. In the summer of 2018, you said,
We will keep cursing monsters lest we begin eating ourselves, and I
agreed. There has been nothing more to remember since. When
they ask me what my name means now, I carry silence
at the ridge of my grisly throat; I remember you
to ask back if they have ever tasted snow.

Black Coffee and Bread

Tony Morris

In the summer of calla lilies and black bears came the yellow, rough cushion of evening. Behind the clouds, lavender, blue, tangled in the red sun setting over the lake, I thought of Lois, soft hands floating above the wood board surface, gritty with cornmeal and starch, a baker's wife I'd met the summer of timber and lakes, long hours working saws and winches, hauling stumps down from the rise, hitching ropes and chains to pulleys.

And at the end of day, calloused hands and coppery smell of blood and sweat mixing with empty fears that nineteen years of mediocrity couldn't explain, I'd wash my hands and face, comb my hair, change my shirt, and hike down to Ninth Cloud Breads, order black coffee and honey-sweetened corn-cake, take a corner seat beside the window, watch the day turn into night, and listen as she hummed a tune I never knew the name of, but somehow seemed familiar all the same.

Then, as the shadows lengthened on the hemlocks, pine and spruce, she'd leave the counter, wiping powdered hands-on apron, smile and nod as if she somehow understood the shape of hard labor on the soul, then sit across from me and talk about her dreams tending garden on the Southend, lips blushed in ocean salt, Tropic of Cancer as the last minutes ticked away before closing when I'd rise, say goodnight, then head back to the trailer, or sometimes to the bar until the weary in my body drove me home, where I'd lie awake and track the cold indifferent stars that spun against the dark outside my window (there must have been a million) while I sweated in the summer heat and wondered, much like today, if the honeyed smell of corn cakes might have made it all complete.

Splintered

Jan Kaneen

"Behold! Creation as it truly is!" So spake the wicked magician as he brought forth his enchanted mirror—evil indeed—for it diminished everything good, and magnified all that is bad in this world. How the magician laughed as he travelled the land showing his terrible truth to all that would look.

"Where's Dad, Muvva?"

The words jolt me out of the fairy story. I close the *Bedtime Treasure Book* and move it into the "to keep" pile. Charley and his thirteen-year-old mates have been talking in mock Cockney all week, but it's early Friday morning and, what with everything else, I've just about had enough. His silvery eyes fizz with mischief as he scatters his breakfast things into the dishwasher.

"I'm not playing this game anymore, Charley," I say.

A wide smile breaks his face in two. He has large features that will be handsome one day when he's grown into them, but today they look awkward, caught in limbo somewhere between childhood and growing up. As I walk past him, he raises his hands so he looks like he's halting a car.

"Whoa, standard banter, Muvva," he chirps.

"Pack it in, Charley," I snap, moving his spoon into the cutlery rack, turning his Keep Calm Play Rugby mug upside down. "You know your Dad was at his Christmas do last night. He probably got sloshed and crashed out on the houseboat."

"Well he hasn't texted me or Sam," he says, packing it in. "Maybe he fell into Regent's canal, drunk, and he's floating face-up, like this." He crosses his eyes and flops his tongue out of the corner of his mouth.

I close the dishwasher and sit back down at the breakfast table. The hotch-potch of items I gathered last night are gathered on the tabletop. It wasn't just a displacement activity. Hugo's been banging on for days about me being like one of those sad hoarders off the telly who fill their empty lives with useless crap by way of compensation. He said I should *let go* of some of my *baggage*.

It is a motley collection to be fair: a chipped pottery seal bought on a childhood trip to Blakeney, pressed violets in a clip frame as a remembrance of that last day with Granny before she started forgetting things, a pink taffeta dressing-up skirt that I thought I'd save for my own daughter if I ever had one. I've kept these things because they hold memories, moments, hopes, but I'm done with all that this morning and toss them into the cardboard box with the rest of the jetsam. But not the *Bedtime Treasure Book*. I run a fingertip over its cover, feeling the embossed illustration pressed into red leather-look cardboard—an indented prince in doublet and hose with tapered shoes and a feather in his hat. He hasn't changed a bit, still holding hands with his wimpled princess, leading her toward their happily ever after. The art deco swirls sing of the 1930s, something I didn't appreciate when I was little, though I always knew it was old, with its battered corners and magical smell. Maybe it's the warmth of my touch that releases it—the scent of cobwebs and coronets, of yesterday.

"Plea-ea-se Granny, can we have one more?"

Lynn asked the same question every night. I could never see her face because our beds were separated by the chimney breast, but I knew exactly what she would be doing, hands pressed together, church-steepled to her lips for maximum impact, begging Granny to read us just one more story.

Granny's reply was part of the fabric of every bedtime. "But it's time to go to sleep, my sweetheart."

"Oh plea-ea-se," we'd chime, a duet now, and Granny would smile and shake her head and open the *Bedtime Treasure Book* to read us just one more fairytale in her low slow story-telling voice.

I pick the book up and let it fall open. It chooses *The Snow Queen* again—of course it does. Grandma must have read us that story a hundred hundred times, and the *Bedtime Treasure Book* has not forgotten. We loved that story so much, for its sadness and antique language, and because the hero was a little girl brought up poor but happy by a loving grandmother.

One day, a small boy peered into the wicked mirror and cried, "But that is not I!"

The assembled crowd looked deeper and saw the truth . . . then the falsehood. They cast the mirror down and smashed it. Alas! For even the smallest splinter was a bane. If one such tiny fragment found its way into a human eye, that sad beholder would be rendered unseeing of anything good, and if one pierced a human heart, that heart would become cold and insensible as a block of—

"Sam, has Dad texted you?" Charley's question tumbles me back.

Sam walks into the kitchen dressed in the self-imposed uniform of his peer group; quiff, super-skinny spray-on jeans and a Jack Wills windcheater.

Rucksack on his back, he's ready to go. He's shorter and slimmer than his younger brother, and he has Hugo's eyes. I catch the warning look he's aiming at Charley, raising his eyebrows then blinking them back to normal before glancing at me.

"No Charley, he hasn't, but he'll be fine. He had his Christmas party last night. He probably got wankered and flaked out on the boat in London like he did on his birthday. Standard Dad."

I wince, partly at the language and partly because of the seen-it-all-before description of his father's modus operandi.

"Can you not say wankered please, Sam?" I say.

"Fair enough Mum. Gotta go now, the bus'll be here in five minutes. Laters."

He turns to leave. A cold, white light streams through the roof lights in the vaulted ceiling, illuminating granite and slate, promising snow.

"Bye love," I call, "Have a good day." Then to Charley, "We'd better crack on too, love, we don't want to be late." I put on my coat and pick up the charity box leaving the *Bedtime Treasure Book* open on the table.

Charley hops out in front of the tall metal sign that says Sancton Dyslexia School.

I wind down the window and call, "Bye love. Don't worry about Dad. He'll be okay." Then I wait, watching as Charley walks down the crowded drive, moving stiff inside his quilted parka, blowing out powdery clouds as he turns to wave. Icy lawns and frosty oaks sparkle clean and crisp as I hear the word *banter* then squawks of laughter before the voices dwindle into the distance. I check the mirrors before setting off and am surprised by my reflection. I thought I was smiling. I let myself relax a little, but the image of Hugo's corpse rises into my mind, floating motionless in the Islington canal. A heave of anxiety rises with it, like morning sickness, and before I know it I'm thinking about birth and death. I pull myself together and press redial on my hands-free. It's the eleventh time I've called Hugo's mobile since two a.m. For the eleventh time, it goes straight to voicemail. He sounds vaguely annoyed as he tells me to leave a message. I don't. I call switchboard at the American bank where he works. An anonymous receptionist tells me what I already know—that he was at the Christmas party last night and isn't expected in until after lunch, and to have a nice day.

"If there's no news by twelve," I tell my reflection, "you'll have to call the police," and I set off home, feeling a little bit better because I've got a plan.

I stop in front of the six steps that lead up the grassy bank to Flag Cottage. Thin swirls of snow are trying and failing to settle on the thatched roof, and the sky-white windows are staring out over the frozen fen. I switch off the engine and remember the first time I ever came here. We'd driven down on the spur of the moment out of Cambridge in Hugo's old Datsun Cherry to see his father through the winding country roads. It was only fifteen miles or so to the little hamlet where Hugo's father spent most of his weekends.

Hugo's undergraduate voice had been quick and earnest as he climbed out onto the unmarked track then looked up at Flag Cottage.

"It's named for the irises," he said. "They grow along the wettest margins of the fen, in golden profusion."

It always sticks in my mind how he spoke. I was so taken with it back then and by his round Cheltonian vowels—so different from the pre-university boys back home in Bolton. No one would dare say words like golden profusion in Bolton, not at the school I went to.

"It's lovely," I said, and it was, its white plaster splashed mauve by an equally lyrical wisteria.

"Like you," Hugo said, quick as sixpence, then he bent to kiss me full on the lips. "Come on, let's go in and see the old man. He's going to be so surprised, and he's going to love you, sweetheart. I just know he is."

Typical Hugo, as I was to find out soon enough—as apt to pop up unannounced as he was to not pop up at all.

I place my hands at ten and two on the steering wheel and reel myself in. Flag Cottage has stood firm on this riverbank, I tell myself, for four hundred years or more. It's seen floods, storms, wars, plagues—things so much worse than this. Then I close my eyes and picture the landscape behind me how it will be in summer when everything's all right again. The River Ouse will earn its lazy name as the willows rustle and chirrup with life. I listen hard, half expecting to hear the summertime thrum, but it's winter, and Hugo's gone missing, and the bare willows are tapping and scratching like old cold bones. I get out of the car and go inside to do the pre-weekend clean, pretending I've put Hugo out of my head.

In the same town, there lived two best friends, Gerda and Kay. One winter's day, when the wind roared and the snow fell, they sat in Gerda's attic, gazing out of the window.

"Look how the snow swarms," said Kay. "Like white bees."

"And do the snow-bees have a queen?" asked Gerda.

"That they do, and sometimes she comes into this village at night to breathe white leaves upon the windows."

That same evening, when Kay was gone home, he warmed a penny and pressed it to the frozen window that he might see outside. As he watched, one great snowflake grew larger and larger until it took the form of a woman with skin of white and eyes of moonlight. She nodded toward Kay and beckoned with a slender finger.

It's noon when I hear the front-door latch click up. I don't need to look at my watch because I've been deliberately not counting down the seconds. I close *The Bedtime Treasure Book* and dash with it still in my hand to the front door. The relief I feel as I see Hugo morphs immediately into something else. He stoops to fit himself through the Elizabethan doorframe and the cold creeps in with him. The willows scratch at fat flakes that are falling thickly now. He leaves the door ajar and walks past me stinking of stale booze. I look outside at his red Jag parked on the verge opposite. He must've braked late because it's too close to the fen drain, jutting into dead scrub. It looks shockingly red against the pale landscape, like arterial blood, and has left parallel tracks of dark green where the tires have disturbed the first covering of snow.

I follow him through the cottage, through the sitting room to the adjoining barn that we've made our bedroom, my heart beating in my head.

"Don't you have anything to say?" I ask, boiling coldly.

"You won't like it." He slumps onto the bed and I remember the day we bought it, twenty-five years ago, a late Christmas present to each other. We'd searched north London for days, braving the weather and crowds to find our "forever" bed. The smiling assistant had told us it was made from oak beams salvaged from demolished cotton mills and I was glad the hard-working wood had been given a second chance.

"I've been done for drunk driving," he says.

I don't mean to, but I fold in half like someone's punched me in the stomach. Wild thoughts swirl and flurry around my mind but I don't let them show. I sit on the sofa at the foot of the bed and listen without interrupting.

He got shit-faced at the party and lost his phone. It was too cold to spend a night on the houseboat, so he caught the train and fell asleep. He woke up at the station and realized his loss. It was three a.m. The cabby's number was in the missing phone and there were no taxis at the rank. He decided to drive and was stopped going too slowly up the hill. He was 178, way over the limit. He spent the night in a cell. They wouldn't let him go until he was sober enough to drive. He walked back to his car and drove home. He's in court on Tuesday.

I keep my face straight because I don't want it to give me away. I don't want it to look like I love him.

"I'm going to find out what this means," I say, taking my phone from my pocket as he lies on his stomach, his head in his hands. "You'd better have a shower," I tell him as I tap at the smart screen, "and take an aspirin, too"

"I'm sorry," he says.

I make my voice calm and deadpan. "I know," I reply, and he jolts his head up to see what I mean, but I'm glassy-eyed. "You told me last time. But sorry isn't just about what you've done Hugo, it's about what you're going to do too—a commitment not to keep on making the same stupid mistakes."

"Don't be so bloody pious," he spits.

When he's gone to shower, I control the tears by putting the phone down and escaping back into the fairytale.

Gerda and Kay were making a snowman when suddenly Kay clutched his eye.

"Let me help," cried Gerda, concerned for her dearest friend.

"Do not fuss " he snapped, lowering his hands. "It has gone." And he frowned, his face hardening. "Oh," he cried in disgust, "you are grown so ugly, uglier even than your ugly snowman," and he kicked it to pieces, laughing at her dismay. Yes, reader! Your guess is right! Splinters from that wicked mirror had pierced his eye . . . and his heart.

The rage comes from nowhere. I drop the book like it's white hot. How could I have ever loved that story? Poor Gerda, doomed to travel to the ends of the frozen earth for months and years, braving witches' spells and impossible odds, risking death and rejection, and for what? Love? Kindness? A happy ending? Hugo was right when he said I should chuck it out. What's the point in happy endings? What about happy here-and-nows?

I take up my smartphone and start tapping in angry jabs. *Hugo's been done for drunk driving again.*

Lynn messages back immediately from the other side of cyberspace. *Oh my God. How many times is that? They'll throw the bloody book at him.* The phone rings before I have chance to text a reply. I answer like we're in the middle of a conversation.

"It's only his second offence for drink driving, Lynn, the others were for speeding, and as far as I can see, they won't count against him now. I'll google it now. Call me back on the landline."

When it rings I hold the receiver between my ear and cheek on a half-shrugged shoulder so I can google two-handed, speaking the words out loud for my sister's benefit, "One previous conviction . . . three years ago . . . breathalyzer score of . . ." It takes a long, long nanosecond to zip through cyberspace and come back with its judgement, ". . . a minimum three-year ban with a £5000 fine."

I hear her breathe in relief.

"Well at least he won't go to prison," she says.

And suddenly, it's too much. My tears fall, not in brave, gentle rivulets, but hot and fast, in red, swollen waves. "He could've killed someone, Lynn . . . and what about the example it sets . . . what if Hugo tries to tell the boys it's not that big a deal . . . what if they copy him when they learn to drive . . . what if they get into accidents and—"

"Oh, sweetheart," she says. "What does he have to do to make you fall out of love with him?"

Hugo walks back into the bedroom with a towel around his waist.

"Sorry, didn't mean to interrupt," he says. "Do you want me to leave?"

The sing-song sarcasm in his voice makes me flash freeze. I tell Lynn I'll call her back, then close the laptop and wipe my face with the heels of both my palms, pulling the skin so tight my eyes stretch into slits that splinter the light into pinprick shards, like hoarfrost.

"Read this, so you know what I know," I say, handing him the laptop, and as he takes it from me our fingers touch. The feeling is so strong it quite takes my breath away. Nothing.

A frozen, fearless nothing, hard as power, cold as freedom. I look up into his face and it's as if I'm seeing him for the first time. How old he has become—pinched and mean, and ugly as the first day of winter.

Aubade

Rayji de Guia

૪

At dawn, you perform
    a reverse striptease
       —boxer briefs, jeans, and white kurta—
  repossessing how we have
      so tenderly unraveled
    in the night. Our illusion ends
without a word. What was there to say
      when we cannot admit
     to knowing? But dearest, I hear you:
    Swift undoing of body
        before returning to your lover
          as you were. December rose
through the window, glamor has fallen, drunken
       rendezvous only remembered. As friends,
   allow me to miss softly, so soon, you
     in yesterday's nakedness, open grace
        in bed, to be offered prayer, to be eaten.
        Now, my throat is empty,
the jamun tree outside my witness.
     Imagine if I said stay. Imagine if I said
     anything. Instead,
I watch you sink in the shadows.
        I want to plead, *Don't be*
         so distant, because farewell is
      the inevitable I try to swallow.

Coronabrain

Ashley Chang

From my room, I can hear Mom and my brother Taylor getting popsicles from the fridge.

Taylor: I miss being able to go out to eat and having options.

Mom: I miss you having friends.

* * *

I introduce myself at the beginning of a virtual conference call.

Me: I think I like dreaming a lot because in my dreams I interact with people.

* * *

It's pitch black outside. Dad and I are in my room, and Mom is by the kitchen.

Mom: I'm going to go spray the hornet's nest!

Dad: Jin!

Mom: I love you!

Dad (to me): You know what 'I love you' means? I'm going to do it anyways.

* * *

Taylor walks into my room and catches me playing Candy Crush while watching my lecture. He walks out, and then, ten minutes later, walks back in.

Taylor: By the way, I didn't tell Mom.

Me: Thank you, you're a good brother.

Taylor sits on my bed and opens his iPad. I stare at his screen.

Me: Your background is Sour Patch kids?

Taylor: Yes.

* * *

I think about a month ago, the night before I left campus. I was talking to my roommate, Kelly.

Me to Kelly: You're the best.

Kelly: You're the best . . . beatboxer.

* * *

Taylor: Mom just has a Mom sense. She knows when you want apples.

* * *

My neighbors ring at our door and leave before we can answer. On our doorstep, we find a poster from them telling us they had hidden plastic eggs in our yard, as an early Easter egg hunt.

Me: You know what's cute but low key still spreads coronavirus?

* * *

Mom goes outside to get the mail. As she walks outside, she points at a cat.

Mom: Taylor, I think that's the cat that bit Julian.

Taylor: That one?

Mom: Yeah.

Taylor: I pet that cat sometimes.

Mom: When?

Taylor: In the mornings, before I get on the bus.

Mom: I think it might be feral.

Taylor: I think it's the neighbor's cat?

Mom: Which neighbor?

Taylor: The one by us . . . the one with the cat.

* * *

Mom walks into my room. I pause my lecture capture.

Mom: Were you playing Candy Crush?

Me: What did you want to say?

Mom: What you can tell people is that the houses are 1 to 2 acres here, so we have natural distancing.

* * *

I have a Zoom conference with my English teacher and start talking about Nerf Guns.

Me: I didn't ever see them until I learned to look.

Teacher: That's a good line, write that down.

* * *

I overhear Mom telling Taylor to do homework and practice the trumpet. Afterwards:

Mom: I'm a little tired.

Taylor: Me too.

Mom: I only got like, six hours of sleep.

Taylor: Me too . . . Ashley did too.

* * *

Taylor and I bike up and down the hill in our neighborhood. Afterwards, we start eating Spam, seaweed, and rice.

Me: Do you ever read a book and not like it because it's too obvious what the author's trying to say?

Taylor: No. But do you ever read a book but can't go to sleep cuz you're thinking about it, and it's 1 AM?

Me: Sometimes.

Taylor: And then you look it up, and it's the seventh book in a series, from seven years ago, and it's the last and there's a cliffhanger. They literally ended it "99, 98, 97 . . . ." That's it.

Me: Isn't it good if they don't tell you everything?

Taylor: It was about clones, Ashley.

Fireworks

C.L. Nehmer

It couldn't have lasted more than a minute
or two—a sudden downpour, passing over the sand
just long enough to wet our picnic blanket,
the carefully packed supper, our card games
and sparklers. Long enough for the kids to look at me
with that helpless look they used to give me
when I would hold them down for vaccination—that look of
why don't you make it stop, a look as if
I could save them, if I wanted to, and why didn't I—
and what can a mother do, but blanket her body
over our vulnerable books and phones?

And I think of another beach, summers away
from here, before moving trucks and tonsils
and stacks of laundry, to the most wonderful wet
of a July dusk, a slower rain that ran in rivulets
down my teenage face, the fuse of his tongue
setting spark to every synapse in my girl body—
rain and mouth and my unsheltered heart
wanting the moments to go on forever
before Mom would pull up and honk the horn
and we would run towards the beacon of those taillights
into the refuge of her waiting car.

The Strength of Strings: A Memoir

Ed Davis

Flinging open the front door, Eugene warns: "Don't come in here without an instrument!"

He needn't worry. I've brought my 1977 Martin D-35 acoustic six-string, a beautiful guitar that has always exceeded my ability to play it. After driving nine hours, my body still hums from the road. I've just driven 450 miles from Yellow Springs, Ohio, to Silver Spring, Maryland, to see my old childhood friend Steve at his son's house. Eugene set up the visit before our mutual pal began chemo and radiation and wouldn't feel well enough for visitors. Steve recently had surgery for glioblastoma, a highly malignant brain tumor. There's no cure; treatment strives to prolong life.

Standing just inside the doorway, a couple of steps down the stairs toward his subterranean suite, Steve looks pretty much as he had the last time I'd seen him twenty years ago, except his beard is more grey than blond, and, like me, he's toting a bigger gut. I hug him, and we three descend to his cave.

The sight of sixteen black instrument cases lined against the wall like coal cars at a siding takes me aback. He's been collecting guitars, banjoes, mandolins, and fiddles for over forty years. I see he's still got the Martin he bought in the early '70's, the guitar that ignited his acoustic career. I smile. In the beginning, there'd been another guitar . . . .

In the autumn of 1965, I was thirteen. Nights had already turned chilly in the highlands of southern West Virginia, and the afternoon breeze was cold. I was on my way home after a day with friends, when the unmistakable sound of an electric guitar floated toward me. I stood in the middle of Mahood Avenue and marveled. The sound seemed to emanate from the rear of the Byrd house and seemed live, not recorded.

Nobody I knew could play the guitar. We longed to, aching to become the next band of working-class kids to seize the world's attention as the Beatles had. So far, lip-synching was as close as we'd gotten. I wondered: should I keep on walking or sneak around back and see who was playing those magic strings? Doing so would mean I'd have to face the music in more ways than one.

Finally, I decided and cut through the Byrds' side yard, slowing as I approached the rear patio. Then, steeling myself, I turned the corner to find an incredible sight: my former best friend electrifying the air with sound. I'm not entirely sure what I felt just then, but it must've been similar to what I'd experienced the day I'd stood up at the end of the sermon in the First Baptist Church, squeezed to the end of the pew and marched down front to commit my life to Jesus. My stomach was almost that fluttery.

Steve looked up.

"Hey," he said.

"Hey," I returned, hunched inside my army jacket at the edge of the concrete slab. The day wasn't as dark as it had been only a couple of minutes ago.

"You gonna stand there . . . or come over?"

I walked over and sat down. Despite the harsh wind of almost-October coming at us across the back yard, some part of what was frozen between us thawed a little while we eyeballed each other above an object whose power I felt in my chest and limbs. Maybe that no-name, sunburst electric had the power to make a nobody become visible in our junior high world. A lot remained to be seen, like: does he hate me?

Now, sitting in Zack's air-conditioned basement, I'm glad to see that my old friend can now fret strings again. We do a little picking—Eugene plays a song by Jason Isbell, whose voice and songwriting we both admire, and Steve joins him on a bluegrass instrumental, "The Red-Haired Boy." After surgery only a few weeks ago, Steve had lacked enough strength on his left side. His progress is heartening. In the morning Zack will drive his father to the doctor in Baltimore to plan his treatment program. Once or twice Steve shows signs of some short-term memory loss, but all three of us aging boomers do. He laughs at his forgetfulness and is once again the friend with whom I've shared a lot of history, not all of it positive, not all of it resolved.

As the early June afternoon wanes, he tells us his disease has been his teacher. "Brain cancer's taught me," he intones, "that if something ain't gonna kill you, then fuck it." Our laughter, some of the best yet, withers to chuckles, then to companionable silence. It is a gift, Steve's humor and post-surgical philosophy. Maybe I drove all that way simply to hoard as many moments like this as I can get before heading back in the morning. But no; I know there's more.

Later, after Zack and his wife Kathy get home and take over as hosts, Steve withdraws to his bed in the next room to recover from what must've for him been a man-talk marathon. Then when he disappears after dinner, missing all the picking that Eugene, Zack and I do in the living room, I understand how thoroughly we wrung him out. Perhaps it was a point of honor with him to last all those hours we demanded his attention. If so, he did a perfect impersonation of himself at 35 and cancer-free.

I find myself beginning to feel closure, like a sermon delivered, a vow undertaken, last call come and gone. While Eugene and Zack play and sing on into the night, I retire to my assigned bedroom, lie on the futon and try to sleep, *need* to sleep if I am to retrace my path home in a few hours. Why is it always after midnight when unfaced demons arrive? I find myself pulled once more back to Mahood Avenue when our emotional landscape was altered forever.

It occurred right after school was out for the summer, between seventh and eighth grades. While I wasn't present, my peers who were there described it to me vividly. Bullies were ubiquitous during my childhood, and Scooter Clark was at least the part-time bully of Mahood. Touch football games tended to break up when he came around, but for some reason, Steve *became* the game that day. Scooter apparently thought it'd be hilarious to dismantle Steve's new bike while everyone watched. The only way my friend could've stopped—no, delayed—the inevitable would've been to fight him, in effect, offering himself as a human sacrifice. But my friend chose (wisely, to my mind) not to challenge the bully; I'm pretty sure the witnesses would've chosen likewise. I don't know how many Mahoodians were there, or whether they tried to discourage Scooter or cheered him on. Doubtless, some onlookers would've loved a fight. But they didn't get to see one that day. At some point, Steve gathered his bike parts and went home.

Where he stayed and was not seen again the entire summer.

The previous summer, Steve and I had been as close as two adolescent boys can be. We listened to "A Hard Day's Night" on the record player in his room that reduced the band to a high-pitched whine, until, finally, it was no longer enough to *listen* to our heroes; we had to *be* them. In Steve's attic, where it was over ninety degrees during the day, we crafted microphone stands from broom handles using coffee cans full of rocks for a base, designed and cut out cardboard guitars: a Lennonesque Rickenbacker for him, a Hofner violin bass for me. Steve's uncle even filmed us miming "And I Love Her" and "I'll Cry Instead," threatening to save the film and show our wives and children in the distant future. We felt far too fab to fret about events so far away.

Although we spent plenty of time as Lennon and McCartney, we hung out with other Mahoodians, too. But after "the incident," I don't recall a single Steve sighting. How he convinced his parents it was normal not to leave the house except when someone drove him somewhere, I have no idea. But he pulled it off.

His peers, though, were another story. In his absence, the prosecution became adolescent-boy savage. All summer my friend was convicted repeatedly for the terrible crime of being victimized by a bully everyone feared. Witnesses to Steve's humiliation became character assassins. Within a couple of weeks, had Steve stuck so much as a toe in the street, sharks would've surrounded him, seeking blood.

Or so I assume. It never happened, allowing the scapegoating machine to continue deconstructing Steve's character, behavior, personality, and appearance. Shredding my former friend became a ritual during downtime between our juvenile delinquent behavior, ranging from shoplifting and shooting out streetlights with bb guns to stealing and drinking beer from Craig's dad's basement. But we always had time for trashing Steve. Scapegoating him must've felt to me at times like my early drinking did—intoxicating, empowering, making me feel I could take on anything (except bullies), because I was in, not out.

It's taken nearly five decades for me to see how badly I failed the greatest test of friendship and basic human decency life had offered me up to that point. In the intervening decades I rationalized my cowardice: how could one as socially marginal as I was, champion anyone—me, a complete follower, barely able to eke out enough self-esteem to get through those awful days of junior high, when a guy could (and did) approach you in the crowded hallway and for no reason knee you hard in the balls?

Steve's ticket back into the club cost him $40 (the price of that no-name guitar), one damned lonely summer and scars I can't imagine. I'm sure none of us apologized. We were young Appalachian males, a demographic not notable for expressing emotions beyond anger. As soon as word got out that Steve could play, he rejoined us without fanfare and we went on as though nothing had happened. By Christmas, we all had cheap guitars and amps from Sears or Montgomery Ward. I wouldn't know for a very long time that something cataclysmic, at least a seven or eight on the emotional Richter scale, had occurred that summer we scapegoated my best friend.

In the immediate aftermath, I don't recall feeling much remorse. That would take years. When I first began writing this essay, I thought it'd be about Steve; now I know it's about me. It's the window through which I look back to make some sense of childhood, or, more aptly, the *end* of childhood. Music became our bridge between that murky period of full-fledged kidness and real adulthood, allowably delayed in America of the '70s and '80. By the next summer, I'd become bass guitarist in a cover band specializing in the Rolling Stones, while Steve got seriously into folk, developing a taste for Joni Mitchell, Bob Dylan, and John Hartford.

During high school, we made a couple of halfhearted attempts to patch what had broken in the summer of '65. We spent an afternoon at my house listening to *Abbey Road* and smoked illicit cigarettes in an alley running parallel to Mahood. But by that time, I was hanging out before and after school with my fellow rockers at Hamden's Snack Bar, a scene that never became his.

Then, in college, while I stayed home and commuted to Concord College, a few miles away, Steve lived in West Virginia Tech's dorm almost a hundred miles away. He'd come home on weekends and teach me awesome songs he'd learned: "After the Gold Rush," "These Days," "The Weight." He also began to compose songs, while I wrote literary analyses. Our new relationship's pattern was set: we'd pull our ships alongside each other, drop the dinghy, row over, share a little conviviality, then return to our dark, separate seas to chase our own white whales: girls, drugs, booze, even academics. I majored in English, Steve in Acoustic Folk (Pre-Bluegrass). I can't help thinking he earned the better degree.

Now, a half-century later, I lie in the house of my old friend's 35-year-old son, trying to sleep, visited by something from the past that's damned hard to articulate much less resolve. But the longer I lie, the more I think I may be getting the answer I've needed. I know that, fifty years ago, I should've walked, as I did down that church aisle, right up to Steve's door in plain view of the Mahoodians, and said, as I did to Jesus, "I will stand by you, friend, come hell or high water."

With all my heart, I wish I'd done that; but I was a follower and took the easier, softer way. That fateful summer I was thirteen, I had the chance to do for my friend what I would've wanted him, our positions reversed, to do for me. Amazingly it has required decades to awaken me to this sad fact and say what I need to say: *Steve, you traveled alone to the heart of the labyrinth, slew the Minotaur, seized the grail, and returned to sing your tale to the accompaniment of a no-name, sunburst, double-pickup electric guitar you bought at Lowe's for forty bucks.*

Lying on my futon, looking backward from the perspective of a half-century, I can't discount the possibility that the incident ultimately meant more to me than to him. I hope so. Tomorrow I might make my belated amends and hope he'll forgive me. It will be easy to request a few minutes alone with him before Zack takes him to the hospital. *No*, says the still, silent voice I depend on since quitting alcohol in 1993, *your obtaining forgiveness is not what's important here. The cup of culpability belongs to* you. *Bringing up something that happened so long ago is a burden your friend doesn't need now (if ever). Wish him Godspeed and go away.*

After that, I sleep.

The next morning, just before father and son leave for Baltimore, I hug Steve and say, "None of us has more than one day at a time." Lame, I know, but after yesterday's companionship and last night's ruminations, it doesn't matter what we *say*. What matters is what we did together yesterday afternoon: talk, laugh and pick without tears of self-pity, remorse, or recrimination. And not one word about when, whether, or where we'd meet again.

Dust

Evan Guilford-Blake

The doves cuddle in the nest as they stare through the bars of their cage, the opened slats of the blinds, the tight mesh of the window screens, into the dismal, sunless morning. They are mystified, it seems; the world is as much a mystery to them as they are to Krista. She watches them while she waits for the water to boil, inhaling the smell of the newly ground coffee: one of her favorite aromas. *Le parfum du rôti français*, according to Gabriel in his silly, wide-grinned, early-morning Romantic mode. One of his favorites, too.

She wakes Tennyson with a kiss and a glass of orange juice. He is the only little child she has ever known—heard of—who likes to sleep in but, this morning, he wakes with a huge smile and throws his arms around her neck, surprising her and spilling a few drops of her coffee onto his favorite pajamas.

"Oops!" he says. "I got Shrek dirty."

She smiles.

"It'll wash out," Krista tells him.

He sits up, takes the OJ and swallows it in one large gulp.

"My," Krista says, "somebody was thirsty."

"*I* was thirsty," Tennyson replies, "not somebody."

Krista kisses him again. Naming their children after other poets was Gabriel's idea. She'd been reluctant when he mentioned it—"Who'd want to be called Hughes, or *Plath*?"—but when he suggested "Tennyson" the idea had grown on her. It was, after all, appropriate for either gender, and there were both singularity and inherent poetry to its sound.

"*You're* somebody all right," she tells him.

"I am?" he says.

"Yup," Krista answers. "Let's get you dressed. We're having bacon and eggs this morning."

"Neat-o keen-o!" he says, echoing Gabriel's favorite phrase. He scrambles from the covers.

"The sky is dirty," Tennyson notes.

"Uh-huh," Krista says as she sips the coffee. Tennyson's appetite astonishes her: Food at 8:00 in the morning repels her, but he eats—as he does most everything else—vigorously. "It's going to rain."

"I don't think the birds like it."

"The rain?"

"The sky. They like sunlight."

"So do I," she says.

"Me too!" Tennyson exclaims.

"Well, we'll just have to order you a whole day *full* of sunlight."

He looks confused. "How do we order one?" he asks.

Krista smiles. "Well, when you get home, we'll write a letter to the Sun and ask him to make tomorrow sunshiny all day. Can you do that?"

Tennyson looks crestfallen. "I don't know how to make all the letters yet, Mommy," he says. "We're only up to 'M'."

She kisses the top of his head. "I'll make all the letters you don't know. Okay?"

He smiles. She loves his wide, toothy smile that looks just like Gabriel's little-boy grin. "Okay!" he says, and stuffs a whole slice of bacon into the smile.

Despite the overcast, he's buoyant in the car *en route* to pre-school. School is an adventure and Tennyson loves adventures. At 9:30 she drops him off, watches him race to the door, and returns home. She prefers to have him with *her* but she's learned that four-year-olds aren't prepared to deal with the concentration demanded for writing. Before, she and Gabriel took turns. Now . . . Well, now is now.

She takes a shower, washes her hair, dries in front of the mirror, looks at herself. "There is nothing wrong with me," she says, then shakes her head. She talks to—at—herself, her reflection, the objects in her life, too often. "That has to stop," she says.

The computer is still on from last night. She sorts through the stacks of papers, disks, pencils, coffee cups, and curiosities that clog her chair, her desktop, and rereads what she has written, makes a minor correction, reads it again, then looks out the window. It's busy: Women with strollers pass, trucks blow their horns, leaves fall. Downstairs the doves are cooing at the top of their oddly powerful lungs. Their cage needs to be cleaned. Her office needs to be cleaned. The *house* needs to be cleaned; domesticity was never her strength and, the past five months, it has become utterly incidental to her life. Everywhere, she is surrounded by dust and disorder. She tries, more for Tennyson's sake than her own; but, she acknowledges, it's a half-hearted effort.

She sighs and stares at the screen, her fingers poised on the keyboard. She types:

As through a dream
The glimmer softens
And there stands

And she stops. And there stands—what? who? Gabriel, of course. But she loathes confessional poems and this has all the symptoms of one. What would he think.

I'd hate it. But it would be a good confessional poem, he says.

She sits back and looks at him. The urn is exquisite. And dusty. She looks at it daily, of course, but she hasn't touched it since she put it on the top of the low bookcase a week after the funeral. It has stayed there, an indelible scratch blemishing the otherwise cluttered but ignorable landscape of her office. Now she gets up, takes a t-shirt—one of Tennyson's—that's draped across a chair, left for some distraction on its way to the laundry hamper, picks up the urn and carefully, slowly, strokes it clean. Then she sits on the chair, the covered gray marble bowl between her legs, and reaches for the lid.

When she first brought the urn home she sat with it, like this, alone, at night, arguing with herself whether to open it, to smell its contents, to touch them. She started to lift the lid—her fingers closed around its spired handle—but stopped. What, after all, was there? Ashes? Bits of bone? Dust, become dust.

That was—exactly—five months ago. The urn has, since, remained on the bookcase in her office, undisturbed. Tennyson has forgotten it: In his youthful resilience, he has adjusted: no nightmares, no recriminations. The occasional "I miss Daddy," but he has accepted his absence. We forget because we must, not because we will. *Wrong, Mr. Arnold*, she thinks, and lifts the lid.

Inside is a small mound of gray-brown-blackness, its contour interrupted by tiny protrusions. She takes a deep breath, then touches one. Bone. But there is no sensation in the contact; it's as insignificant, as asymbolic, as the residue of last night's chicken.

She lifts her finger to look at it. It's no different. Flesh, soft and unsullied. She reaches down again; this time, her left index finger probes. She lifts it. There, on the tip, are specks of the gray-brown-blackness. And suddenly she is terrified: *What can I do with it?* she thinks. *I can't wash it off, it's part of Gabriel. But I can't leave it on; Tennyson will see it.*

He won't mind, Gabriel answers.

She stares at it. She tries to think: *It's just so much dirt. It's not Gabriel.*

No, it's not, she hears him say.

Keeping her index finger extended, she closes the urn and replaces it on the bookcase. She stares at the finger. The ash is still there. Should she just blow it away and get on with her life? Krista shakes her head. It *is* Gabriel.

You think so. Hmh. You *really* think so?

She sighs, and sighs again. What will she do with the rest of the day? She can't type, she can't read, she can't wash the dishes.

She goes downstairs. Sappho is in the nest; Catullus is standing beside it, preening her. They need baths; it's been three days since she sprayed them. She can do that! If it were sunny she'd lug the cage outside, but the rain looks imminent. Using her right hand, she gets the water bottle and opens the cage door.

The doves look unconcernedly at this intrusion into their sanctuary. She's had them for six years now; a wedding present from one of their close friends (who thought they were a pair, not just a couple; "Sappho" was intended as irony), and they are as unaware of *her* as they were the day they arrived. But, if they're not affectionate, neither are they perturbed by her presence. With her clean hand she reaches in, presses a finger gently against Cat's chest, and says "Up." Obediently (or instinctually, she's never been sure which) she hops onto Krista's finger. She moves her just below the perch; Cat hops up and onto it. Saph stares—longingly, Krista thinks: The doves dislike any separation.

She sprays Catullus through the bars of the cage. She blinks, lifts one wing, then the other, tucks one leg and stretches both wings in what Krista calls the birds' Tai Chi routine. Clearly, Cat enjoys this. So does Sappho, but her bath will have to wait until Cat replaces her on the eggs. If there is one thing they are deadly serious about, it's caring for their eggs. That, in the six years, not one has hatched is irrelevant. Hope springs eternal in their soft white breasts, too. The thing with feathers.

So there is the rest of the day. One-handedly, Krista pours more coffee, drinks it, watches her left index finger as if it's ordained that the ash will somehow envelop the rest of her hand, her arm, her body. Despite her shower she feels unclean. This tiny fleck of residual love on her finger has scratched her soul, leaving its faint tarnish.

"It would be easier if I could cry," she says to the coffee cup. The therapist told her there was nothing wrong with that, that it was, in fact, the best thing she could do. But tears, on the rare occasions they've come, haven't helped. She wants to cry *out*: *Why*; but she's done that, too. And there's been no answer forthcoming. She and Tennyson will sit in front of the television on

Saturday mornings, watching cartoons, and the coyote's car will crash into the side of the mountain, and it will spring up to chase the roadrunner again (like a grinning Gabriel, pretending he was driving a car, chased a howling Tennyson around the room), and Tennyson laughs; and Krista smiles but she can feel the tautness at the corners of her mouth. People do not spring up. They lie among the ruins of the car and the dust along the road, and they will never chase anything again.

The morning has managed to pass. She's finished four cups of coffee and is a little wired. In an hour she can pick up Tennyson. But in the meantime, there is still the matter of her left index finger. The ashes remain, reminding her vaguely of the wedding ring she decided she couldn't wear any longer, but which left its impression for weeks after she took it off.

She sits at the dining table, the breakfast dishes still on it; she can see into the living room, where books, magazines, newspapers, the occasional blouse or pair of shoes are randomly piled or left, in an abstruse pattern of loneliness. She watches the doves. On the wall is their wedding picture: Gabriel and Krista, his curly tresses flowing over his collar, her straight hair severely short. They are smiling, both dressed in white: His tuxedo, her gown. *We looked so happy*, she thinks.

We were, he says.

"Were we?" she asks the picture.

Of course. Newlyweds are always happy.

"That was then."

His smile broadens. She squeezes her eyes in disbelief, and when she looks again the picture is exactly as it was.

Wash it off, he says. You won't ever be renewed, but you'll be fresh. -Ened

"I can't," she says.

He recites for her:

> *I struggle towards the light; and ye,*
> *Once-long'd-for storms of love!*
> *If with the light ye cannot be,*
> *I bear that ye remove.*

"Matthew Arnold did not have all the answers, Gabriel!"

And *you* have them?

"No." She sighs, sees that Saph has left the nest and Cat is settling in, gets the water bottle, coaxes the smaller dove to the perch and sprays her. She thinks Sappho almost smiles as she fluffs her feathers, discarding the motes of dust, the bits of seed among them.

The clock strikes one. *The mouse ran down*, she thinks in honor of Tennyson's favorite nursery rhyme. She opens the door to find the day surprisingly warm and—expectedly—muggy, gets an umbrella, her bag, the keys. She decides she will take Tennyson for pizza, a special treat. Besides, it will be another hour she doesn't have to face—this: She looks around the living room, the dining room, the staircase. All the places she lives her life.

Krista stands at the door, still wondering what she will do about the ashes on her finger. She can see them, clearly; she uses her right hand to lock the door, to open the car, to put the keys into the ignition. She drives that way to the pre-school. As she turns in she hears the thunder. She sees Tennyson standing among a group of children under the canopy of the walkway. She waves, but he doesn't see her.

She parks the car in the lot and, as she walks the hundred steps to meet him, there is a flash of lightning and another thunder roll. *Damn it*, she thinks, *I left the umbrella in the car*. She waves again and calls his name. He turns and calls "Mommy."

The rain breaks just as she reaches the covering. He runs up to her, gives her a big hug and pulls a large manila envelope from under his shirt. "Look!" he says. "I made it."

He holds the envelope as, with her right hand, she opens the clasp and gently slides out the crayoned construction paper. On it, there is a neatly drawn picture of a roadrunner, a mountain, and a man in a car. A lump comes to her throat. "That's very nice," she says.

Tennyson points. "That's Daddy."

"I recognized him right away," she says.

"You did?"

"Yup." She looks at her son, closes her eyes a long moment. Behind them she sees Gabriel, hears him murmur, but though she listens as hard as she can, the words are indistinct.

"Mommy?"

"Yes, sweetheart?"

"Are you okay?"

She opens her eyes. "Absolutely. Hey, how 'bout some pizza?"

"Neat-o keen-o!" he says and looks into the rain. "Then can we go home and write the Sun the letter?"

"You, *bet*." Krista breathes deeply and stares into the downpour. She tucks the envelope carefully into her bag and says: "Let's go!"

They walk briskly through the rain. With her right hand, Krista holds Tennyson's small left hand. She reaches out with her left and lets the water spill across it.

what is Art

Kym Cunningham

maybe it's metaphor between
night(i.e.) hiked overhead
blood like a shield
w/hole organ vacuumed

maybe it's my hips grinding
exposing caesura in bone
in(di)visible womb belies

maybe it's intestinal (in)discretions
suture's seepage sealed
that marrow kiss

maybe it's the widening amidst
my fist in your space
ribbons edged to present

my lips&mouth
that vessel leak/ing
against hooded siege
to insure disease

pelvis to dust
words congealed on a p(a)late
decay underneath

in lineage's secret(e) release
in steward of memory-to-be
connecting human&beast

your slackened jaw
ripping tongue between
the gaps in your teeth

maybe it's you finally letting me speak

Singultus

Ann Kathryn Kelly

I hiccupped and slid into the booth beside Shelly.

"I'm late. Sorry."

I wiggled out of my down coat. It was March, slushy, with a bite in the air. Colleagues Tina and Shelly joined me every Thursday for happy hour.

"We got chicken nachos, they should be out any minute," Shelly said.

I hiccupped again and she rubbed my back. "You alright?"

I'd drawn in a big breath. Holding it, I turned to her and nodded. I pointed to Shelly's pint glass when our server approached. Exhaled. "The same, please."

Our server dropped a coaster. "Comin' right up."

I hiccupped again.

"You sure beer's the answer?" Tina asked, eyebrow raised.

A hiccup is a spasm of the diaphragm; a quick, involuntary inhalation, a pause in airflow, a catch in the throat as the epiglottis closes. A resulting short, sharp sound.

Hic!

They're not often cause for concern. Many of us take in too much air when talking, some of us drink or eat too fast, and who doesn't suffer from belly bloat at times, especially around the holidays?

The etymology can be traced to the 1500s. Even earlier medieval spellings include *hickop*, *hicket*, and *hyckock*.

The French spell it *hoquet*, the Danes, *hikke*, the Swedes, *hicka*. It's *hick* in Low German, *hipo* in Spanish, *hikuk* in Persian, and *hikka* in Bengali. The Italians? *Singhiozza*. Proof that everything not only tastes but sounds better in Italian.

Used in a sentence, hiccup can describe a minor interruption, a company's financial performance, a car's reliability.

Examples:

Beth is convinced it's a mere hiccup in the young couple's marriage. Nevertheless, she's thrilled to have her daughter home.

There's been a hiccup in this quarter's earnings.

The car engine hiccupped, but wouldn't start.

Hiccup is a wonderful example of onomatopoeia. *Achoo, ahem, belch, buzz, fizz, glug, hum, pop, purr, squish, zap.*

Among the folk remedies suggested to try stopping them:
Hold your breath.
Pinch your nose.
Breathe into a paper bag.
Swallow a teaspoon of sugar.
Pull your tongue.
Rub your eyeballs.
Bite into a lemon.
Drink from the far side of a glass.
Scare the person hiccupping.

Tina heaped nachos onto her plate and scooped guacamole from a plastic cup. "You'll never guess what happened the other night." She shoveled a forkful, chewed, and raised her thumb. "Mmmm!" she nodded.

Twenty minutes into our night, I was still hiccupping. I flagged our server again. "Can I get some water?"

Shelly waited for Tina to stop chewing. "What happened?"

Tina stabbed a piece of chicken. "I was in the parking garage getting my keys out of my bag when some guy came out from behind a car. He was coming straight at me, not saying anything, just walking fast."

Shelly's eyes widened. "What'd you do?"

"I wasn't sure if I should get in my car and lock it, yell at this guy, or call someone. I was still figuring it out when he jumped the hood!"

Our server returned with my water as I stifled hiccups.

Shelly put her fork down as Tina waved us closer. We bent our heads over the plate of nachos.

"He grabbed me," she whispered, "and said . . ." She locked me into her stare and stretched the silence.

"Boo!" she yelled, banging her fist on the table.

Shelly shot upright, her back hitting the padded booth. A hiccup seized in my throat, my heart thrumming. Tina burst out laughing.

"What the hell is wrong with you?" Shelly massaged her heart. "People are staring."

Tina grinned. "It worked, didn't it?"

The medical term for hiccups is *singultus*. Those lasting minutes are common and *transient*. Those lasting hours, even a day or two, are less common and *persistent*. Those lasting more than a month are uncommon, highly distressing, and *intractable*. Intractable hiccupping can cause exhaustion, dehydration, acid reflux, irregular heartbeat, depression.

When are hiccups serious?

When it might be gastroesophageal reflux.

When it might be related to bowel or gallbladder diseases.

When it might be pancreatitis.

When it might be hepatic metastasis, a fancy term for liver cancer.

When it's a side effect from chest or stomach surgery.

When waste products accumulate in the blood from kidney malfunction (uremia).

When it might be alcoholism.

When a brain tumor interferes with the breathing center.

"Nonstop hiccupping," the surgeon explained, "can be a clinical sign of a disorder affecting the brain stem."

I sat across the desk that June afternoon, studying this doctor, trying to block out his words. My brother, Sean, sat beside me. The March evening with my friends in the pub was the start of what would become an almost daily occurrence; sometimes in thirty-minute increments, sometimes for hours.

My brother, eighteen months older, was chauffeur, medical transcriptionist, therapist, head cheerleader, and sponge in the room as we cycled through hospitals that summer. It started with a CT scan. From there, an MRI. Soon after, I was referred to a specialist.

I was forty, unmarried, without children. Sean and I lived within ten minutes of each other. Running interference for me, as the baby in the family, was something he'd been doing all his life along with brothers Pat and Tom.

As we listened to the surgeon, Tina's garage story popped into my mind. I needed her there to bang her fist on his desk. Tell him to stop this. Now.

Drugs listed to treat intractable hiccups include:

Chlorpromazine, an antipsychotic. Used to treat schizophrenia, bipolar disorder, severe behavioral problems in children, nausea, vomiting, anxiety, symptoms of tetanus—and, intractable hiccupping.

Baclofen, a gamma-aminobutyric acid agonist. Used to treat spastic movement disorders—spinal cord injury, cerebral palsy, multiple sclerosis—and, intractable hiccupping.

Gabapentin, an anticonvulsant. Used to treat seizures, anxiety, insomnia, hot flashes, alcohol withdrawal, as a mood stabilizer in bipolar disorder—and, intractable hiccupping.

"You have a neurovascular disease, a cavernous angioma," the surgeon said.

He explained a cavernous angioma can resemble a raspberry. Affected vascular walls become thinner, weaker, bulge out in clusters, fill with blood. After each bleed, he continued, the cavernous angioma flattens out. Over months, sometimes years, it refills, resembling again a raspberry cluster that will rupture, flatten, fill. Rupture, flatten, fill.

Rupture, flatten, fill.

The brain stem, we learned, controls breathing and heartbeat. At just three inches long and an inch-and-a-half wide, it resembles a human thumb. In the weeks following my diagnosis I'd ruminate on the strangest things, like how most of the shoes in my closet had heels higher than the length of my brain stem.

The brain stem coordinates yawning, swallowing, coughing. Vision and hearing. Facial movements. Balance and body coordination. It manages pain sensitivity, alertness, awareness. It was a part of my anatomy I never considered, and one I would never again take for granted.

"Based on your scan," the surgeon said, "I believe your angioma has a high likelihood of hemorrhaging again."

My mind raced. *Good Christ.* A squeezing sensation, hot and twisting, wrapped around my stomach.

"When?"

"Maybe a year, eighteen months. Maybe only six."

"Can this kill me?"

He paused. "It's the repeated bleeds over time that add up. Each hemorrhage compounds symptoms and can lead to stroke-like deficits." He glanced at Sean before looking at me again. "With an aggressive angioma like yours, I strongly advise you to consider a craniotomy."

Shave my hair, slice my head open, and start poking around? I visualized Dr. Frankenstein bending over his table. Me, on it.

"But if I do nothing, will this kill me?"

He studied me from across his desk. "We don't want to let this continue."

The squeezing stole my breath. A white-hot flush raced like a thermometer up my neck and into my face. Sensing how his answer affected me, he forced a note of optimism.

"Image-guided surgery has made removal safer."

It wasn't only hiccupping that had led me to that exam room. I yawned in unstoppable stretches. I'd been dry heaving for months, gagging upon waking. Bile, yellowish-green and slimy, burned my throat. Headaches raged, my eyebrows feeling like they'd been slammed with a mallet. Muscle weakness crept into my left side, most noticeable in my foot and ankle; in time, moving up my leg and eventually putting me into a brace.

"How many patients have you operated on who had this?" Sean asked.

"Don't worry." He turned to address my brother. "I've seen it before and I can get it out."

My stomach heaved. Did that mean, regardless?

All brain surgery patients, he pointed out, require some combination of physical, occupational, and speech therapy. Some need assistance regaining gross motor skills, sitting or walking, for example. Fine motor skills may be affected, things like grasping objects. Many, he cautioned, can develop issues with balance, speech, or swallowing.

"We set the expectation that the first year after surgery is the most critical. What you don't recover in that year may never come back."

He stopped, his eyes softening. His back, straight as a rod, rounded as he leaned forward. In that moment, it seemed he saw me for the first time.

Does he realize his words are sharper than any scalpel?

The exam room had collapsed in on me. The ceiling and fluorescent lights seemed within inches of my head. My voice was tiny, unsure. Unlike me. "Maybe I should get a second opinion?"

He nodded. "It can't hurt, though I think you'll find most surgeons will agree. Your angioma is not going to stabilize. You've had too many bleeds, and that indicates to me it will happen again."

He stood and extended his hand. "Talk it over with your family. If you decide on surgery, we should get it on the calendar. Sooner, not later."

"I can't do it," I said to Sean in the car. "I won't consider it."

"Let's get a second opinion, Annie."

I didn't want another opinion. I had plans, a dream safari to Kenya coming up. I'd gotten into my first home several years earlier and was rehabbing it, bringing my Victorian back to its glory. I couldn't afford time off for surgery. There were porches to be rebuilt that summer, and insulation to be blown into walls before winter.

The surgeon told us the brain stem's width is about the size of an American half dollar coin. When I got home that afternoon, I dug through a desk drawer. My Aunt Gloria had given me a half dollar years earlier for our nation's bicentennial. I found the coin, tucked in the back of the drawer. I studied it, looking at President Kennedy's image above the dates 1776-1976. I found a ruler and measured across. It was, by a hair, just under an inch-and-a-half wide. The surgeon's words on what the brain stem controls flooded into my mind.

Breathing. Heartbeat. Consciousness.

Why do humans and mammals alike hiccup?

Scientists theorize hiccups may be a carryover from our evolutionary past. That the muscles engaged may be related to amphibian gills we had three hundred million years earlier that enabled breathing in lakes and oceans by closing the glottis and expelling water; an involuntary survival mechanism made redundant when we moved from water to land. Others suggest hiccups help unborn babies strengthen breathing muscles; that fetuses, at eight weeks, can hiccup.

It's a question without a definitive answer.

What is known is that *singultus*, in Latin, loosely translated means, "to catch one's breath while sobbing."

There were times when deep breaths were hard to pull in, times when sobbing would have been an understandable reaction. I fought it, stoically weighing options. I agonized over what I may be left like, with surgery. I brooded on the deficits that could come, without it. An endless tug of war.

Mostly, I prayed.

I put the half dollar back into the drawer, opened a Google window, stared at my computer. Minutes passed. The cursor blinked. My hiccups punctuated the quiet.

I typed, 'Brain surgeons in Boston.'

An Open Letter to the Secretary General

Stuart Stromin

Your Excellency:

I am writing to you today as the authorized representative, empowered by the unanimous consent of my constituents, of a recently founded non-profit organization, CANEM.

CANEM is the acronym for Canine Association for Normal Exercise and Moderation, and I am honored to hold the title of President. Our group has been constituted to provide a timely conduit to a better understanding between our species, particularly in response to recent developments, which have impacted our community.

It seems apparent that the human populace has undergone a recent and unique transformation, resulting in a startling and welcome change in the human behavior to which we have become accustomed over many centuries of cohabitation. In all this record of contact, we have accepted human filth, insensitivity and acts of wanton destruction with a resigned grace as an inevitable norm. The basic hierarchical needs of shelter, food, and protection, notwithstanding the delight of our legendary companionship, are among the many advantages we each accrue from our interaction, which persuade us to an indulgence of human faults, and, in fact, we have become accustomed to them. It cannot be argued that the natural world has seen dramatic improvements in the last few months, and for that we must be grateful. Skies and water are cleaner, all living creatures are finding the planet a better place.

Among humans, we find, of late, a more dog-like behavior in many ways, such as a newly appreciated discovery of the pleasures of lying on the couch, a more deliberate day-to-day pacing free of the typical freneticism, longer sleeping periods, increased feeding patterns, and, in particular, an unusual fondness for walks.

It is the subject of the frequency of these walks that has prompted this urgent and rare communication.

Most of our canine members are comfortable to walk humans once or twice a day. Beyond that, it is hard to maintain the same enthusiasm, energy, and vigilance. You may not be aware of the effort involved to secure a perimeter against the possibility of unfriendly animals, to sniff out the distinctions between friend and foe, to guide our subjects along the route, and many other subtleties of what may seem like simple perambulation. In addition, we are obliged to retain our alertness while restrained and distracted. For the totality of our recollected history, dogs have always been the initiators of the daily walks, insisting morning and night with barks, scampers and other signals to draw their human companions out into the elements, rain or shine, in an effort to keep them healthy and well-balanced. We have accepted this duty with dogged ebullience, and will continue to do so, as our historical alliances with the human species endure, but we cannot remain muzzled. We respectfully request some moderation to curtail this mileage to a restrained level, so we may preserve some of our stamina for our roles as comfort pets to bring you emotional support through your current crisis. In short, having to monitor you twenty-four hours a day, we are exhausted.

I urge you to convey our sentiments to your species, and hope that with some modest adjustments on your behalf, we may continue our long cooperation to reciprocal benefit.

Yours faithfully,
Rex Taylor
President and co-founder of CANEM

PS: Please also consider recommending that humans take a trip to the groomers.

This is to Say

Andrena Zawinski

I want to say

it was serendipitous
at a drive-in
in the backseat
of a cherry Chevy,
gravelly speakers blaring
an actress' struggle
to render Wordsworth's
splendor in the grass
of glory in the flower

want to say

it was exhibitionism
bobbing in the water
seaside, sun blaring down
on Atlantic City kids playing
gold diggers in the sand,
parents spinning wheels
and turning over cards
at casino tables

to say

it was ever so natural
on the farmhouse back porch
wrapped in the itch
of horse blankets
everyone else asleep,
only snorts from a herd
of whitetail deer
edging the corn field
delivering a warning

I want to say

it was simply irresistible
unwrapping the scarf
unbuttoning the blouse

loosening the skirt
letting them drop in a heap
to the hungry earth,
flushed by the heat of day
having waited so long
every pore willing.

I do not want to say

it was against the will
head shoved down
into the groin,
sound turned up
muffling cries

do not want to say

the new bikini
was torn from the hips,
mouth bruised
coughing gasping
for air

not to say

the deer ran off
the corn bowed down
husks crackled under feet
pounding ground,
the scarf tied tight
across the throat
the blouse and skirt
lost to the maze

to say

the face was masked
in backseats, in deep waters,
the wild fields, struggling
to breathe   to breathe
        to breathe in
    the long dark night.

Hers

Jocelyn Williams

I have seen her weep.

That time, music blasting from his car stereo, did she fall off the bridge or did her brother threaten to tell? She splashed and said come get me boys, but her broken bones were ugly to them.

Tears land like knives or laughter.

I love her room with its mirrored closet doors and the satin cover, sweet and strong, like dying apples. I plan my skin to grow into her blouses, hung neatly.

She scrubs cups until they sing, scraping black bits off sheets used to bake thinly sliced potatoes or molasses cookies cut square because she doesn't leave room.

Then come blue tunes of adultery. From the root word, I gather it means to grow up. She asks was he there? Were they laughing? I hear her tears in the mirrors. She turns up the volume. She doesn't reach for my bare back.

She stays the same the next day and the next and again on repeat until there's just a mattress. Stripped, I no longer hold the edge with her.

I part my hair down the back, finally straight, as I tell myself in the mirrors, I will get a bike next summer. She doesn't know. In seven, I want more.

Tears land like knives or laughter.

The table is always round, always covered with waxy white lace, folded back, to make room for sliced bread in a wicker basket or butter and whole milk and jars of mustard pickles. Later, a tape deck and ashtray and cards, scrolled with red in hands chapped the same color. Glasses of dark rum and bottles of beer, gathering to witness her lose or grab a blade.

At night, the B-side over, it's her laughter at the door. I hear her up against the frame and a guy say where then? They must fall. She leaves the glass for morning and crawls in beside me instead, her summer breath warm and right on my neck.

That winter, it's not her turn. The one after, a new guy leans against the door like a gun or her brother. I'm not crying. Go then, she says. I reply. I like their mirrors whole and the boyfriend drives me.

In summer, I'm on top bunk. They have my arms pinned. Ssssshh, they are saying, you had a nightmare. I have known them for five days. Together we have memorized the words to as many songs. I tell them it's my mother, and they believe me. It's been a year since I slept near her.

She's in the hospital. I don't visit. The doctors are telling her to lose her leg. She's saying she cannot: she's too young. How will I dance, she asks, find a man? She has been turning on her motorcycle for a married guy on a crew, all of them in yellow hats. Her leg, from the knee down, tears like a love letter.

Tears land like knives.

There is a photograph of laughter or her brother in a white tee with a smoke in his mouth, his hair slicked. A second of her getting married in a pretty pink dress. I hide them in a dictionary. A year later she tells me they were stolen. I let her believe this. (Her brother died driving and drinking. She was seven months pregnant.) I keep these.

She's in the hospital. I have seen her weep. I don't visit.

I feel guilt at night when I take my shirt off, clean enough, and don't hang it. Even if I do, it doesn't look the same. My sheets are cold. I vow to make things seem more hers, the room at least, not much more.

Sometimes I turn off the music. I stand at the sink, still and dry-eyed. I begin washing the mustard-now-juice glasses, free of their past, of knives, of laughter. I push suds to the side like I am the snowplough, threatening to bury us.

Freiheit

Samantha Pilecki

It's all set.

By the end of the day, David Gray will either be dead, in solitary, or on his way to freedom. But he has to go *today*. While he's got scrubbed, semi-fresh smelling skin and a shave.

Plus, there's a shipment coming by automobile today. That means the guards will be distracted. They won't see his face. They'll see a suit. They'll see a burgher businessman, going about his day. Nothing special. Nothing remarkable.

Not a prisoner of war.

Hallo Leutnaunt. (Hello, Lieutenant.)

Einen schönen tag noch. (Have a nice day.)

Gray steps out of his room. He tries to hold onto all the German he's learned, but it leaks from his brain, as if from a sieve.

He puts one foot in front of the other. He's wearing the same knee-high boots he's worn since leaving the base at Le Hameau, but he's let out the side seams from his trousers so they could be worn over the Royal Flying Corp issued boots. It was time-consuming, ripping stitches with a fork and re-sewing the dirt-crusted material with Kennard's smuggled sewing kit.

Hopefully, it's been worth it.

The soles are worn thin and the toes are battered to bacon, but for all the blessed world they look like normal shoes. *Civilian* shoes.

Hallo. Einen schönen tag noch.

Hopefully, he can remember his lines.

Gray's boots *shmuf* over the smooth, wooden floors of the prisoners' quarters. He pushes open the large door, stepping down into late-spring sunshine, thankful for the prison Commandant's indulgent ways. The POWs are only lightly supervised, waiting in line for snacks from the canteen, or gathering round a wrestling match, or setting up self-made chess boards in the Yard.

Excuse me. Not the Yard. *Die Spielplatz*, Gray corrects himself, in German. He can't begrudge these lads passing the time as pleasantly as they can, but at the same time, he can't stay here.

Because this is the *great* war. The war to *end* all wars. And he's got a job to do, even if it kills him.

Which it most surely will. But it's 1917, and not just any man can fly planes. Gray knows he's killing other country men, good British boys, by being idle here at Camp Crefeld. When he could be serving Queen and country.

Gray doffs his hat, a stupid black bowler which gives his face a comically dour air, but POWs can't be choosers. If this hat is what Dear Old Mam was able to smuggle past the package line, in a nutcake tin, then this is the hat he'll wear. He scratches his head, puts the hat back on.

All part of the disguise.

Last night, he folded down the collar of his RFC coat and pinned it flat, in imitation of an actual suit. He even stripped the gold braids from his cuffs, cut the medals from his breast, and gave it all to the Frenchie. Gray's got the forged papers, the German marks, and the map, folded flat in his pocket, like armor. He's got the German words on his tongue. That's all he'll need.

Hopefully.

Camp Crefeld's high stone walls beckon, magnet-like, and Gray walks. He switches his valise, heavy with emergency tins of food, to his right hand, palms sweating.

The truck's not there. The guards still stand at rapt attention.

Gray stops to pretend to check his non-existent pocket watch, looks up into the sun. It will shine whether he is free or not. Whether boys go over the top and die, or planes get shot down. Whether men are left to rot, unspeakably alive with half their innards on their outsides.

Stupid, smiling sun. In this moment, Gray hates it.

Danke schon, Herr God.

Kennard, the man with the sewing kit, walks by, but doesn't slow down. He acknowledges Gray with the barest of exchanges, a nod that conveys respect rather than comradery. Gray raises his own chin, and turns away, abruptly, towards a noise at the gate.

The truck is there.

It's hissing steam and smelling of fumes, and the Germans are all over it, questioning the driver and admiring the machine, still a wondrous novelty. There's stacked wooden boxes, full of supplies, tarped down in the back bed. Young German boys dawdle over unpacking them, eager for an earful of how much *wasser* to add when *der motor ist überhitzt* . . . .

Gray is astounded at how much of the conversation he understands.

"*Papiere, Herr?*" A guard, distracted by the driver's story, flicks out a lazy hand towards Gray. Gray complies, taking the necessary identification from his breast pocket.

He tries to quell the tempest in his chest.

"Einen schönen tag noch," the guard says, hardly glancing at Gray's papers. Gray stuffs them back into his pocket, wonders if he should ask a question about the auto, but decides it would be foolish. That it would be like tying on Icarus wings of wax.

"Danke, mein Herr," he offers humbly, and moves past the auto.

Moves past the guard. Past the gate.

Moves past Camp Crefeld.

Stalks of uncut grass slap Gray's knees, but he is floating, untethered to the path cutting towards town. The noise, the smell, the *there-ness* of Camp Crefeld, recedes, replaced by springtime shoots of newness. By dark dirt and dense forest.

By quiet.

Eventually, Gray's heart stills, and the nervous drumroll steadies into a semi-victorious tattoo. He takes the map out of his pocket, consults the timetables.

The Dutch border, and its freedom, is 18 miles away. There's a tram stop up ahead, and Tram 88, heading north, is due soon.

He picks up the pace, hoping to God he looks like a German civilian intent on making his tram, instead of an escaped British prisoner.

The only thing between him and a bullet is the clothing he wears.

He reaches the tram stop, a shady, deserted pavilion, made of white painted lumber. Gray walks to its flimsily promised safety. He's made it past the guards, yes, but he hasn't made it to freedom. He hasn't reached Denmark, hasn't reached . . . He consults his map again.

Breklenkamp. Yes. That's the name of the Dutch town, on the border. Just past the Nordhorn stop.

Freedom. *Freiheit.*

Gray traces the roads he must take, one final time, as the tram tugs to the stop. Its mechanisms slow with a wheezing *chuf,* and Gray looks up, patting down the lapels of his newly pinned jacket.

Nothing special. Nothing remarkable.

Here is his second test.

"Hallo. Wie viel kostet Nordhorn?" he asks, hoping he hasn't butchered the accent.

"Fünfundzwanzig," the operator grunts.

Gray ducks his head, pawing through his marks while trying to understand the cost of the fare he's been quoted. Before too much time goes by, he simply takes a large mark out and asks for change, which he gets, and then gets a seat.

The tram jerks to a start again. Gray crosses his legs at the knee, looking out the open window as the miles roll by. He must be 17 miles away from the border, now.

Had it really been this easy, all along? A uniform tailor-turned suit, a clutched handful of German words? Good Lord, if only he could tell Kennard!

But he's not free, not yet. Maybe 16 miles now. Gray takes out his map again. The Nordhorn stop is seven miles from Breklenkamp and the border, and seven miles is walkable. This far north, the guards are bound to be lenient, less rigorous. Venlo, the town to the west, would be a more obvious escape route, and heavily guarded.

Gray folds his map away. He's making the right decision, with Breklenkamp.

The day darkens into a grumpy, stormy gray, and he feels a tug of certainty, of some divine reassurance. Maybe God hates the sun too, and this is His way of showing Gray he will succeed.

He will be *freiheit*.

The clouds grow heavy and break as the tram tugs further north. Rain thrums over the roof. Wind gusts in through the windows, and Gray rolls up the glass. But if the weather keeps this way, getting soaked is inevitable.

Piddling price to pay for freedom. Rain can't hurt him.

"Nordhorn!" calls the driver.

Gray doesn't bother to thank him as he ducks out into the crashing clap of thunder, the now-pounding rain. The reprieve of the tram departs.

Seven miles.

All he has to do is find and follow the railway line. Gray squints into the stormy onslaught. Spies the rail line. Stalks towards it.

Gray swipes rainwater from his eyes, marching doggedly. At least the weather has deterred any late-night strollers who might cause trouble. Who might stop him, ask questions.

Es tut mir leid. (I'm sorry.)

Ich bin verloren. (I'm lost.)

None of these replies are adequate.

No matter. He doesn't need words, right now. All he needs is seven miles behind him, between him and Germany.

It's miserable slogging through the soaked country. His toes tap the rails, boots worn thin and growing damp. But the warmth of freedom—of Breklenkamp—grows closer with every step . . .

There! A signpost, silhouetted against the soft lights of a town, just over the crest of marshy field. It won't do to consult the map again, it'd be drenched to paste in the rain, but maybe he can get his bearings, check his mileage against his memory, once he reads the sign and learns the name of this misty, glowing hamlet.

Gray hurries closer, heedless of the mud slicking his calves. Of the rain disfiguring his bowler. Of the pins flying loose from the stubborn, British lapels. None of it matters, not now. He nears the carved wooden sign.

By God, it says Breklenkamp!

Gray pounds through the mud, no longer a burgher businessman but a drenched desperado. Soon, he spies an awning, stretching over a wide, lamp-lit outpost. Seated soldiers loll, rolling tobacco, chatting. Gray practically skips down the length of hill.

"Hello!" No need for the German now. Gray crashes into their light, dripping, chest heaving. The Dutch soldiers regard him, rabbit-like, no doubt startled by his sudden entrance. Gray swallows. The English feels thick in his throat, just as uncomfortable as the dry German he's coughed up. "My name is Officer David Gray. I'm a British pilot and was imprisoned at Camp Crefeld."

The Dutch soldiers look to one another. An older man, Gray's own contemporary, stands.

"You are escape prisoner?" he asks, the English heavily accented.

"Yes."

"*Armer mann. Bekam verwirrt,*" the soldier mutters.

(Poor man. He got confused.)

The first taps of fear rattle Gray's rain-chilled spine.

Something's not right. This man's speaking German. Not Dutch.

And Gray is a *poor man.*

Nothing special. Nothing remarkable.

The soldier stands, revealing the enemy bars and medals beneath his overcoat.

"There are two village with name Breklenkamp. One *Niederländisch . . .* Dutch . . ." The man waves, abstracted, a matter of minutes or miles. Who can tell. ". . . one . . . German." He points to the soil beneath his feet.

Gray sinks, sinks, knees soaking in the wet earth, and it's like being shot down all over again. His clothes are shabby, insubstantial. Wearing them is like flying a plane, all the while ignoring it's only coated canvas and wire.

Today was the day.
He's either dead or going back in solitary.
But he's not free.

Off-Kilter Haibun
On May 14, 2020

Jennifer Grant

The same day Lewis and Clark departed to explore the wildness of the northwest, my canine co-pilot and I prepare for our own expedition. Our *Corps of Discovery* does not disembark from Camp Dubois outside St. Louis, Missouri but a cleared-out college town in North Central Florida. Lewis and Clark's goal was the Pacific Ocean. Mine is less grandiose—a mere 58 miles straight away to the Gulf of Mexico.

Boat-less and Unmoored

With a red and white Igloo cooler in the front seat of my borrowed blue Honda and Indiana Jones (with his favorite beef bone) in the back, I am ready for the trek west. Sixty-three days of quarantine has me longing for greener scenery. The sun is already high and hot and I think I should've shoved off sooner. Clark said in his journals that it was cloudy that morning in 1804 when they were *fixing for a start*. They didn't leave Camp River until 4'oclock. Lewis and Clark travelled in a 55-foot keel boat. My ride has a cracked windshield and is 196 inches from nose to backside.

In Pursuit of Adventure

It's nearly 20 minutes into our journey before my second in command, Dr. Jones, and the traffic settle. Then the rhythm of purple and yellow pansies prancing roadside and ditches dotted with wading snowy egrets soothes. An osprey winds its way through the slash pines, leading me deeper into nature's nest and further from fear of a virus that could ravage my asthmatic chest. But death looms near Otter Creek as I spy a grey faced coyote, lifeless on the road's shoulder. Just beyond, on a corner, a couple in white surgical masks sells shaved ice snacks the same color as the blood pooled around the poor dead hound's head.

Viral Pioneer

As I contemplate my own fate, my trusted navigator (my phone), announces my destination on the right. It's here that Capt. Carl of Cedar Key offers me a grin and his grouper catch for today.

> *This spring pandemic*
> *where nothing is black and white*
> *except my Shih-tzu.*

The Mouth on the Mountain

Virginia Watts

This spring, a pandemic has gripped our globe, centering its bullseye on the human life form. Facing a new normal under government-ordered quarantine, we are no longer moving on top of the earth's surfaces as we used to. Meanwhile, on social media, the paintings of Edward Hopper have become more popular than ever. Suddenly, our world has taken on a Hopperesque appearance. Familiar, but emptied. The same, lone figure trudging up and down asphalt past our mailbox. A neighbor bent over in her garden on the mornings that arrive without rain. Her red sun hat, a brilliant, bobbing poppy.

Hopper's paintings depict what a person might be able to recall about a cluttered canvas if asked to describe it years later. We can only take in so much. The color of the sky that one afternoon, a back porch, a man formally dressed in shirt and tie reading a newspaper, his habit, a wife standing straight-backed nearby, one hand on a post, looking far into the distance, not smiling. It's all you need. If you really want to boil us all down to a single drop, we are all basically happy or unhappy at any given time.

The world is unhappy together this spring. We want the return of a social existence, the details of our lives, and most of all, we want humankind to stop suffering and dying from this disease. A phrase often repeated now: *There is always a light at the end of a tunnel.* At the moment, we are not sure how to find the light at the end of the tunnel, or when we should expect to spot the first glimmer.

Growing up traveling the Pennsylvania Turnpike in the back seat of my parents' car, I rode through my share of mountain tunnels. The Allegheny Tunnel, The Tuscarora, The Lehigh, The Rays Hill, and the twin tunnels near the city of Pittsburgh, The Kittatinny Mountain Tunnel and the Blue Mountain Tunnel. The twin tunnels were back to back tubes with only a short break of the outside world separating them. I'd cheer at the end of one, a long ride in and of itself and then, BAM! We were deep inside another mountain.

Even though a tunnel's black mouth on a mountain base became a familiar sight, it remained a marvel. *Explain it again*, I would say to my father. *How did we drill though an entire mountain? Isn't a mountain very heavy? How does a tunnel stay open? Why doesn't the mountain simply crush it in?* He would try to explain the civil engineering of tunnels, how a continuous arc spreads the load, how they are reinforced with different materials such as metal anchor bolts, but as our car spun closer and closer to that mouth, it felt more like a roller coaster car climbing to the top of the first, steep hill.

Like a sudden vacuum seal, the plop of a bell jar over an African violet, entering a tunnel stamped out a sunny day, stopped falling snow, vanished rain drumming on the car roof. My father's elbow would bend. The windshield wipers would fall and lie still.

The side walls inside the turnpike tunnels were covered in shiny white tiles. Like fine glazed china that had lost its way in the Industrial Age. At intervals, the white was stained a coppery brown. Water dripped and sometimes poured down some segments. Too much flowing water made me glance up at the tunnel's ceiling, then ahead for light. Was the mammoth world above—the forest, the houses, the barns, the streams and their boulders—finally breaking though?

As we motored through, the white lights along the ceiling on either side of the car morphed into a Twilight Zone experience, melded into arrows that turned around and launched themselves back at the front of our car. I'd blink, and they would turn back into nothing but lighted boxes over our heads. Then it would happen again. A successful optical illusion. Hypnotized by a tunnel? I could believe that.

During one of these excursions, my father pulled into a rest stop for gas and *a stretch for our wooden legs.* Inside the gift shop, along with other souvenirs of the State of Pennsylvania such as Liberty Bell pencil sharpeners and Amish people salt and pepper shakers, I noticed a rack of postcards, some of the Pennsylvania Turnpike tunnel entrances. No people, of course. Just the tunnel's maw on a mountain bank, maybe a car or two entering or leaving. Only a few different hues to complete the scene. The sky one shade of bright blue. All white clouds. Trees and foliage either forest green or lime green and inexplicably, a deep shade of rose dropped in here and there. Very Hopperesque. A parallel reality. True life distilled.

I was puzzled. Who would send a postcard of a tunnel entrance? Maybe if that was the only way to get back home, a way of communicating I miss you, or I forgive you, or will you forgive me and come back home? Maybe the card might remind someone of childhood days sitting in the back seat of a car, windows open, hair blowing, heading for a visit with grandparents, an uncle, cousins, falling asleep later on the way home, lulled by the rhythm of the open road.

On the flipside of the postcards: "Various tunnels take travelers through the formidable mountains of Pennsylvania." I thought that was very unfair. It sounded like our mountains were meaner and scarier than mountains in other places. Of course, they weren't. They were beautiful, and they let us pass through them safely.

Edward Hopper painted railroad tracks entering the mouth of a tunnel in his work entitled "Approaching a City." In the sky beyond, tall city buildings of beige and grey and one pumpkin orange. No people. No train cars. But the tunnel is wide open. You are welcome to come inside. Yes, you will find yourself in a strange land. Your current weather and customary views will be slicked away temporarily. Your clouds and your sky, your moon and your sun, hidden from view. Even though this is not a place you are used to, you must take this journey. There is no other way to go. Keep looking for the light.

Bacopa Poets & Writers
2020

Renee Agatep writes of her rust belt beginnings in Ohio and now lives in St. Augustine, Florida. Renee earned her master's at Northeastern University and is currently studying English - Literature at the University of Central Florida. Her poetry is forthcoming in *The Texas Poetry Calendar*.

William L. Alton's work has appeared in *Main Channel Voices, World Audience*, and *Breadcrumb Scabs*, among others. He has published a collection of flash fiction, two collections of poetry, a memoir, and three novels. He earned both his BA and MFA from Pacific University in Forest Grove, Oregon.

Rachel Amegatcher is a young author who is excited to continue her writing journey and hopefully not get lost along the way. She does, though, like this quote: "Some beautiful paths can't be discovered without getting lost." After years of scribbling in her journal, this *Bacopa Literary Review* work is her first public piece.

Justin A.W. Blair graduated from the University of Florida in 2005.

Tuhin Bhowal's poems have appeared or are forthcoming in *City 7 Press, mutiny!, Chaicopy, Bengaluru Review*, and elsewhere. Winner of The Great Indian Poetry Contest 2018 sponsored by the On Fire Cultural Movement, Tuhin is currently the Poetry Editor of *Bengaluru Review* and *Sonic Boom Journal*. Tuhin tweets poems @secondhandsins.

Sarina Bosco is a chronic New Englander.

Virginia Boudreau is a retired teacher living on the coast of Nova Scotia, Canada. Her poetry and prose have appeared in a wide variety of international publications, including *Palette Poetry, The New York Times, Claw and Blossom*, and *Grain*. New work will be appearing in *Sunlight Press, Westerly* (Australia), and *Cricket Magazine*.

Caitlin Cacciatore is a queer writer and poet who lives on the outskirts of New York City. She believes poetry has the power to create change and brighten lives, and wishes for her work to be an agent of forward motion. Caitlin prefers writing in the hours just after dawn.

Kurt Caswell's newest book is *Laika's Window: The Legacy of a Soviet Space Dog*. He teaches writing, literature, and outdoor leadership in the Honors College at Texas Tech University.

Ashley Chang is a writer of humor and nonfiction from Forest, Virginia.

Alison Clare is a recent graduate of Loyola Marymount University where she completed her masters in English. She lives in Los Angeles with her bearded husband, baby daughter, and two neurotic rescue dogs. She is a voracious reader and, when her time comes, she will most likely meet her end crushed under the tower of books on her bedside table.

Cynthia Close, armed with an MFA from Boston University, plowed her way through several productive careers in the arts, including instructor in drawing and painting, Dean of Admissions at the Art Institute of Boston, founder of ARTWORKS Consulting, and president of Documentary Educational Resources—a nonprofit film distribution company. She now claims to be a writer.

J. Brent Crosson grew up in Gainesville, FL. He is a scholar of Latin America and the Caribbean and Assistant Professor at the University of Texas-Austin. His critical nonfiction has appeared in a number of journals, and his book *Experiments with Power* is published by the University of Chicago Press.

Kym Cunningham, having earned her MFA from San Jose State University in 2016, is currently pursuing her PhD in Creative Writing at University of Louisiana-Lafayette. Her essay collection, *Difficulty Swallowing*, was published by Atmosphere Press in 2019, following the publication of her poetry chapbook, *l'appel du vide*, in 2018.

James D'Angelo is an attorney and mediator working in Philadelphia. This fall he will start his journey earning an MFA in Creative Writing at Western Michigan University.

Ed Davis's stories and poems have appeared in journals such as *Leaping Clear, Metafore, Hawaii Pacific Review*, and *Stoneboat*. His latest novel, *The*

Psalms of Israel Jones (West Virginia University Press 2014), won the 2010 Hackney Award for an unpublished novel.

Rayji de Guia was a resident at Sangam House in Bangalore. She received First Prize in the Poetry category of the 2nd Gémino H. Abad Awards for Poetry and for Literary Criticism and Second Prize in the English Short Story category of the 69th Carlos Palanca Memorial Awards for Literature.

William Doreski has published three critical studies, several collections of poetry, his work has appeared in many print and online journals, and he has taught at Emerson College, Goddard College, Boston University, and Keene State College. His most recent books are *Water Music* and *Train to Providence*, a collaboration with photographer Rodger Kingston.

Chris Gilmore has a Master's in English Literature and Creative Writing from the University of Toronto, where he won the U of T Magazine's Short Story Prize in 2017. His first book of short stories, *Nobodies*, was recently published by Now or Never Press, and his writing has appeared in *McSweeney's, The New York Times, Canadian Notes & Queries, Hobart, Broken Pencil, Matrix*, and *The New Quarterly*.

Janna Grace has been published in *Rat's Ass Review, Otoliths*, and *The Opiate*, among others. She teaches writing at Rutgers University, and her debut novel will be published through Quill Press in 2021. Janna is the editor of *Lamplit Underground*. Twitter: JGEarthworm

Jennifer Grant resides in Gainesville, FL, where she writes, edits, practices and periodically teaches yoga. Her first collection of poetry, *Good Form*, was published by Negative Capability Press in 2017, and a tiny chapbook, *Bronte Sisters and Beyond*, by Zoetic Press in 2018. Her chapbook *Convergence* will be published in Fall 2020 through Blue Lyra Press. She's been nominated for Best of Net and Pushcart awards. jenniferlynngrant.com

Paul Grindrod is a gardener, birder, and naturalist who's been teaching about nature and science since 1994, with an emphasis on birds of prey. With extensive experience in natural history interpretation in a variety of settings, he is happiest outdoors.

Benjamin Guerette is a teacher from Connecticut whose work was most recently published in *Notre Dame Review* and *J Journal* and given Special Mention in the 2020 Pushcart Prize anthology.

Evan Guilford-Blake's prose and poetry have won 27 awards. His works include the novels *Animation* and *The Bluebird Prince*, and the award-winning story collection *American Blues*. His plays have won 47 competitions; 33 are published. He and his wife (and inspiration) Roxanna live in the southeastern US.

Patrick Cabello Hansel's debut book of poetry *The Devouring Land* was published in 2019 by Main Street Rag Publishing. His second collection, *Quitting Time*, is forthcoming from Atmosphere Press. He has published poems, stories, and essays in more than 60 journals, including *Isthmus*, *Ash & Bones*, and *Lunch Ticket*.

Joshua Jones lives in Maryland, and his writing has appeared in *The Best Microfictions 2020*, *The Best Small Fictions 2019*, *The Cincinnati Review*, *CRAFT*, *Juked*, *matchbook*, *Paper Darts*, *SmokeLong Quarterly*, *Split Lip Magazine*, and elsewhere.

Jan Kaneen has an MA in Creative Writing from the Open University. Her stories have won prizes at *InkTears* and *Scribble*, and the Ely Prize for Fiction. Her debut memoir-in-flash, *The Naming of Bones*, is forthcoming from Retreat West Books in April 2021. She blogs https://jankaneen.com/ and tweets @jankaneen1

Ann Kathryn Kelly lives in New Hampshire's Seacoast region. She's a contributing editor with *Barren Magazine*, works in the technology sector, and leads writing workshops for a nonprofit serving people with brain injury. Her essays have appeared in *X-R-A-Y Literary Magazine*, *Moxy Magazine*, *The Coachella Review*, *Under the Gum Tree*, and elsewhere.

Lisa M. Kendrick lives in the heart of Norfolk, Virginia, with her twin daughters. She has been teaching high school English for twenty-five years; publishes a high school literary magazine; writes curriculum, young adult fiction, and poetry; and performs spoken word. She has most recently been published in *Sister Stories, Red Weather, Moonstone Press, River River, Other Worldly Women Press*, and *Appalachian Heritage*.

Nora Kirkham is a poet and writer from Maine with a Master's in Creative Writing from University College Cork in Ireland. She enjoys writing about human relationships and wild landscapes.

Cal LaFountain's audiobook *Puddle Is an Ocean to an Ant* is out now on Xocord. His cut of the cloud is callafountain.com.

Una Lomax-Emrick is a writer based in Rhode Island and California. She writes nonfiction prose and studies drama.

Mark Gregory Lopez was born and raised in a city by the sea. He earned his BA in English and Bachelor of Journalism from the University of Texas in Austin. His poetry has appeared in *Juked, The Maynard*, and *Borderlands*. He's currently an MFA Poetry candidate at Columbia University.

David B. Maas has attended poetry open mics and workshops, led panel discussions, and hosted poetry shows in the Gainesville, Florida, area for almost 30 years. He is producer and host of The Word Is Spoken. His work has appeared in *Bacopa Literary Review* and other exemplary journals.

Mickey "The Flying Busman" Mahan's poems, after three decades behind the wheel of a transit bus, writing WHILE he drives on a pocket-size memo pad, pen-in-teeth (he calls his writing practice "Writing On The Edge Of My Seat"), have raised an itch the driver's seat can't scratch. So, away they go!

Cadence Mandybura's fiction has been published in *FreeFall, NōD*, and *Gathering Storm*. She won first place in *FreeFall*'s 2016 Annual Prose Contest for her story, "Timestamp." Based in Victoria, BC, Canada, Cadence practices martial arts and plays Japanese taiko drums when she isn't writing. Learn more at cadencemandybura.com.

Bruce Meyer is an award-winning author or editor of 64 books of poetry, short fiction, flash fiction, and non-fiction. He lives in Barrie, Ontario.

Tony Morris has previously published four books of poetry, including his latest, *Pulling at a Thread*. Other publications include: *Spoon River Review, Hawai'i Review, Southern Poetry Review, River Styx, Meridian, The Sewanee Theological Review, South Dakota Review, Connecticut Review*, and others.

C.L. Nehmer is the author of *The Alchemy of Planes: Amelia Earhart's Life in Verse*. Her work has appeared in *Southern Poetry Review, Pedestal Magazine, Southword*, and other journals and anthologies. She was a 2019 Best of the Net nominee. Learn more at www.clnehmer.com or on Instagram @clnehmer.

Hailee Nielsen lives in Ann Arbor, MI. Her work has appeared in *Smokelong Quarterly*.

J. Nishida, sometimes host of Gainesville's Thursday Night Poetry Jam, has been a student of science, education, language, linguistics, literature, and has worked as an English teacher, library story lady, mom, and with nonprofits supporting arts and education. Her poem "Admirable Men" was published in the 2019 *Bacopa Literary Review*.

Yongsoo Park is the author of the novels *Boy Genius* and *Las Cucarachas* and the essay collection *The Art of Eating Bitter,* about his failing one-man crusade to give his children an analog childhood.

LA Patterson is a licensed massage therapist and intuitive healer. She lives in Gainesville, Florida, with her husband and their giant Pomeranian.

Samantha Pilecki's work has appeared in numerous publications, including *Kansas City Voices, New Lit Salon Press, Yemassee*, and *The Timberline Review* (forthcoming). She is the winner of *The Haunted Waters Press* Short Story Competition, *The Writing District*'s monthly contest, and was a finalist in the *Writer's Digest* short story contest.

Rachel Poteet is a second-generation hillbilly, writer of too-serious poems, too-silly plays, and too-many novels. She lives in Blacksburg, Virginia.

Stephanie Powell is a poet based in London who grew up in Melbourne, Australia. In 2019 her poetry collection *Strange Seasons* was published by Enthusiastic Press in the UK. Her poem "The Episcopalian Church car park" in this issue was written during the ongoing COVID-19 lockdown 2020.

Mayneatha Royal refused to harbor negative feelings about all she saw growing up on the southside of Chicago, using her experiences to paint her own picture of strength. Growth is the major influence for all her poetry, and she lives her life's journey as it unfolds, creating beauty out of the madness, each poem written with hopes that someone somewhere will read her work and have the courage to overcome, too.

Jon Shorr is a retired college professor whose creative nonfiction and journalism have been published in magazines, literary journals, and anthologies, including *JMore Living, Tricycle, Passager, Pangyrus, Stories That Need to Be Told,* and *The Inquisitive Eater.*

Kate Grace Smith is a writer and teacher from the south of England, currently based in Madrid. She holds a BA in English Language and Literature from King's College London, and has spent most of her time since graduation on the road.

Krystal Song is a first-generation immigrant with roots in Hong Kong and Shanghai. She works in product in the high-tech industry and currently lives in California. Her work touches on themes of migration, intergenerational trauma, and collective memory and history.

Matthew J. Spireng's 2019 Sinclair Prize-winning book *Good Work* is forthcoming from Evening Street Press. A 10-time Pushcart Prize nominee, he is the author of two other full-length poetry books, *What Focus Is* and *Out of Body*, winner of the 2004 Bluestem Poetry Award, and five chapbooks.

Stuart Stromin is a South African-born writer and filmmaker living in Los Angeles. Educated at Rhodes University, South Africa, the Alliance Francaise de Paris, and UCLA, his work has appeared in *The Chaffin Journal*, *Garfield Lake Review*, *Sheila-na-gig online*, *River River*, *Immigrant Report*, *Blood Puddles*, and others.

Lisa Taylor is the author of four collections of poetry and two collections of fiction. She will have a new poetry collection published in 2021. New fiction or poetry will be or has been published recently in *Lily Poetry Review*, *Tahoma Literary Review*, and *WomenArts Quarterly Journal*.

Siamak Vossoughi, a writer living in Seattle, has had stories published in various journals, and his first collection, *Better Than War*, was published in 2015. His second collection, *A Sense of the Whole*, will come out in Fall of 2020.

Virginia Watts is the author of poetry and stories found or upcoming in *Illuminations*, *The Florida Review*, *The Blue Mountain Review*, *The Moon City Review*, *Permafrost Magazine*, *Palooka Magazine*, and *Streetlight Magazine*, among others. A finalist in 2020 Philadelphia Stories Sandy Crimmins Poetry Contest, winner of the 2019 Florida Review Meek Award in nonfiction and nominee for Best of the Net 2019 in nonfiction, Virginia resides near Philadelphia, Pennsylvania.

Jocelyn Williams is an academic and creative writer who has taught literature at universities in Eastern and Western Canada. She was born in the Maritimes but lives in the Prairies and continues the conversation about women's texts, national narratives, trauma, and body.

John Sibley Williams is the author of *As One Fire Consumes Another* (Orison Poetry Prize), *Skin Memory* (Backwaters Prize), and *Summon* (JuxtaProse Chapbook Prize). A 23-time Pushcart nominee and winner of various awards, John serves as editor of *The Inflectionist Review*, teaches for Literary Arts, and is a poetry agent.

Alexis Wolfe lives in Berkshire, UK. She has been published in *The London Reader, The Wild Word, Spelk Fiction, Lucent Dreaming,* and *New Flash Fiction Review.* Her writing has been shortlisted in various writing contests. Twitter: @LexiWolfeWrites

Cooper Young is a mathematician and poet who hails from Santa Cruz, California. His most recent work has appeared or is forthcoming in *The Wayfarer, Lucky Jefferson, The Albion Review,* and *Miramar.* His new chapbook, *Sacred Grounds,* was published by Finishing Line Press in May, 2020.

Andrena Zawinski's third and recently released full poetry collection is *Landings.* Her poems have received accolades for free verse, form, lyricism, spirituality, and social concern. She is Features Editor at PoetryMagazine.com and founded and runs the San Francisco Bay Area Women's Poetry Salon.

Bacopa Editors
2020

Mary Bast's creative nonfiction, poetry, and flash memoir have appeared in a number of print and online journals; and she's author, co-author, or contributor to eight nonfiction books as a PhD psychologist. Mary offers writing tips and promotes *Bacopa Literary Review* contributors on our Editors' Blog. She is also a visual artist (www.marybast.com).

J.N. Fishhawk is a Florida-born poet and writer whose work appears in a variety of print and online publications. He is the author of two poetry chapbooks and *Postcards from the Darklands*, ekphrastic poems accompanying artwork by Gainesville, FL, artist Jorge Ibanez. Fishhawk and Johnny Rocket Ibanez debuted their first-in-a-series children's book *Billy & Tugboat SallyForth* at WAG's Sunshine State Book Festival in January, 2020. jnfishhawk.com, fishhawkandrocket.com

Kaye Linden holds an MFA in creative writing and is an award-winning writer and creative writing teacher with many publications, including *Tales from Ma's Watering Hole, 35 Tips for Writing a Brilliant Flash Story*, and *35 Tips for Writing Powerful Prose Poems*. She is currently working on her second novel. Visit Kaye at www.kayelinden.com.

Stephanie Seguin writes fiction and humor that have appeared in various journals and anthologies. Currently she is trying her best to write and exist while raising two small children in a pandemic. Some of her past work can be found at www.stephaniesays.net.

James Singer III is a graduate of the University of Florida. He writes short stories and lives in Gainesville, Florida with his wife and two gray cats.

Printed in Great Britain
by Amazon